REFLECTIONS
ON THE
COLUMBIA DISORDERS
OF 1968

David B. Truman

Copyright © 2008 Edwin M. Truman

All rights reserved

ISBN 978-0-557-03118-4

*To his great-grandchildren
Elena Cecilia Truman,
David James Truman,
Malcolm Truman Woollett &
Jessie Elinor Truman Woollett*

This is their history too!

*Tracy P. Truman
Edwin M. Truman*
November 2008

CONTENTS

	Preface	vii
	Prologue	1
1	Introduction	9
2	Why Columbia?	21
3	"The Students"—Who Were They?	57
4	Encountering Parents	89
5	The Faculty in Crisis	97
6	The Presidency in Crisis	133
7	The Trustees as Crisis Managers	163
8	The Mayor and His Entourage	179
9	Black Politicians on the Spot	191
10	The Police: Pro and Con	199
11	The Media: Local and National	211
12	Why 1968?	225
	Epilogue	237
	Remarks at Columbia University October 23, 2003	239
	David Bicknell Truman June 1, 1913–August 28, 2003	263
	References	277

PREFACE

My father, David Bicknell Truman, died on August 28, 2003. He was beloved by his family and admired and respected by almost everyone with whom he had contact over his 90 years, including many whom he never met. He lived a long and fascinating life, contributing importantly to the transformation of the field of political science. He was a full-time academic administrator from when he became dean of Columbia College in early 1963 until 1978, when he retired from the presidency of Mount Holyoke College.

He and his wife, Elinor Griffenhagen Truman, spent 19 almost entirely happy years at Columbia University and were devoted to the institution. Their life on Morningside Heights ended in the aftermath of the tumultuous events of the spring of 1968.

Twenty years later, in December 1988, my wife Tracy and I gave my parents a computer for their 50th wedding anniversary. Soon thereafter, my father sat down at the computer and started to write this memoir. I am confident that he had already outlined the structure of his argument. He reported that my mother, ever his super-efficient research assistant, had carefully clipped and saved many press reports from the spring of 1968. Working at his own pace, he finished a first draft in 1992.

REFLECTIONS ON THE COLUMBIA DISORDERS OF 1968

He sent the draft for comments and reactions to a few friends and former colleagues. He was interested in whether it could be published. He received many favorable comments, but on the question of publication the view was that the draft would require a great deal more work before any publisher would seriously consider it. He made some revisions, including adding the "prologue" with its timeline of events leading up to the spring of 1968 and of the events themselves. He completed this memoir in essentially its present form in 1995, had a few copies bound for family and friends, and sent copies to the Columbia University archives, and later to Mount Holyoke College with his professional papers, with instructions that the manuscript be accessed only with his permission.

In 2001, I persuaded my father to allow anyone with access to his oral history interview in the Columbia archives to have access to his manuscript as well. One reason he agreed was that he thought that his manuscript came closer to telling the full story from his perspective.

After his death in August 2003, acting on behalf of my mother, I directed a number of people to the Columbia archives and my father's memoir. They included Jonathan Mahler, who wrote a short piece on my father in the *New York Times Magazine* in which he mentioned the manuscript.

With my mother's permission and encouragement—she died on April 20, 2005—Tracy and I decided to make the manuscript more generally available. Tracy scanned every page into our computer and I made some corrections. I wrote to *Columbia College Today*, the alumni magazine of Columbia College, and to *Columbia*, the alumni magazine of the university as a whole, offering to provide to people copies of the resulting document at the cost of reproduction. We have

PREFACE

distributed more than 100 copies in this manner. A Columbia College graduate, Frank Sypher, who was also my Trinity School classmate, immediately suggested self-publication. Later, Mark Rudd, who figures in the events of 1968 described in this memoir, made a similar suggestion.

This year marked the 40th anniversary of the events of the spring of 1968. Many commentators now describe that year as a watershed in U.S. and world history. For example, *Time* Magazine published a 40th anniversary special "1968: The Year that Changed the World." Columbia marked the anniversary with a conference and the screening of a preliminary cut of Paul Cronin's documentary *A Time to Stir*. The documentary was reviewed by Paul Hond in *Columbia*. This led to additional requests for copies of my father's memoir and a family decision to embark on this project.

With the support and advice of our children, David Robert and Christine Jane Truman, Tracy retyped the manuscript. As a team, we also checked a few facts, corrected typographical errors, and gave the manuscript a thorough scrubbing. Had my father worked with a professional editor, the published work could have been very different. From the beginning, however, our goal has been to leave his memoir essentially the way it was when my father stopped work on it in 1995—to treat it as an historical document preserving his voice.

My father was 75 when he first started to write. He wrote with the benefit of his own hindsight, but also as a political scientist and veteran academic administrator. From this perspective and experience, he wrote about Columbia and other colleges and universities during the three decades from World War II to the end of

REFLECTIONS ON THE COLUMBIA DISORDERS OF 1968

the 1970s, on the tragic events at Columbia University in 1968, as well as on the U.S. global social and political environment in the late 1960s. At the end of the memoir, we added remarks from the memorial service held for my father at Columbia University on October 23, 2003, and a brief biography of his life.

My family and I hope that the reader will enjoy each aspect of the resulting memoir. We thank Marla Banov, Michael Bradfield, Mary Brown, Madona Devasahayam, Helen Hillebrand, David Howard, Susann Luetjen, Jill Martyn, Isa Hunningher North, and Robin and Tappan Wilder. We could not have completed this project without their encouragement, suggestions, help, and advice.

Edwin M. Truman
Town of Somerset
Chevy Chase, Maryland
November 2008

PROLOGUE

The events with which the present memoir is concerned were rooted in and were inextricably influenced by what was happening nationally in the year 1968, especially in the first six months. That year was, from almost any perspective, one of disorder and even disaster. As Clark Clifford observed, quoting William Manchester, it was "the year that everything went wrong." (Clark Clifford, *Counsel to the President*, New York: Doubleday, 1991, p. 554) He was looking at the year from the viewpoint of the Johnson administration, but his characterization could be adopted by many for whom those months were filled with anguish.

A simple chronology of the most prominent of those events will refresh memories and provide a backdrop for those that are the primary concern of these pages.

On *January 4*, Senator Eugene McCarthy announced that he would enter the New Hampshire Democratic presidential primary to be held in March. President Johnson had not announced, but his supporters were active.

Two days later, on *January 6*, Senators Eugene McCarthy, Robert Kennedy, and others put pressure on the administration to halt the war against the North Vietnamese in order to test the sincerity of their offer of talks. The senators especially emphasized the desirability of a bombing pause.

On *January 30*, the Tet offensive began in Vietnam, in which attacks were launched against 30 South Vietnamese cities, including Hue, Saigon, and the American base at Kesanh. The attackers suffered enormous losses and technically a defeat, but their ability to stage an offensive of this scale, reaching even into the U.S. embassy in Saigon, was a shock to American opinion and reinforcement to critics of the war.

On *March 9*, General Westmoreland called for 206,000 more troops to be sent to Vietnam.

Four days later, on *March 13*, Senator McCarthy won 40 percent of the vote in the New Hampshire Democratic primary. As an officially undeclared candidate, President Johnson received a majority of the vote as a write-in candidate.

The next day Senator Robert Kennedy announced that he was reconsidering his decision not to seek the Democratic presidential nomination, and on *March 17* he announced that he would seek the nomination.

On *March 31*, in a peroration to a speech on the war that was not part of the advance text, President Johnson announced that he would not seek re-election to the Presidency.

Five days later, on *April 5*, the Reverend Martin Luther King, Jr., was assassinated in Memphis, Tennessee. This shocking event was followed by widespread rioting and disorder in many cities. President Johnson called for a national day of mourning on April 7, the day of the King funeral.

PROLOGUE

During the ensuing weeks what Clifford has described as "the war's widening poison" spread not only in the United States but in Europe as well. (Clifford, *Counsel to the President*, p. 554) It was especially dramatic in France, where a general strike, on *May 12*, brought out hundreds of thousands of workers and students, and on *May 27*, the French government barely survived a censure vote of no confidence by a margin of only eleven votes.

Mixed, one might say entangled, with these developments were the disorders at Columbia. That the latter were a part of the larger complex of actions is suggested by Clifford's discussion of "the growing sense of social and political crisis," in which he says, "On April 23, a student uprising at Columbia University began a new cycle of violence on the campuses of America...." (Clifford, *Counsel to the President*, p. 536)

The Columbia disorders of April and May were preceded by a string of less dramatic, less consequential events stretching back almost three years.

In the *spring of 1965*, the annual dinner awards ceremony of the Naval Reserve Officers' Training Corps (ROTC) was disrupted and driven indoors.

On *November 15, 1966*, a campus building was entered in order to protest and obstruct a recruiter for the Central Intelligence Agency (CIA), thereby registering a demand for a ban on CIA recruiting on the campus.

On *November 22, 1966*, the Students for a Democratic Society (SDS) entered Low Library and demanded a public debate with President Kirk on student rights and on the University's "involvement" with the military. (The "debate" was held.)

REFLECTIONS ON THE COLUMBIA DISORDERS OF 1968

In *April 1967*, officer recruitment by the Marines was disrupted in John Jay Hall, but was resumed in another building the next day more or less without incident, thanks in considerable measure to the efforts of a number of the faculty.

This was succeeded, in *November 1967*, by a referendum among all College students which supported the policy of open recruiting by a ratio of two to one.

In *December 1967*, at the request of the College Faculty and after pressure from the SDS, a presidential committee was appointed to develop guidelines for Columbia's connections with outside agencies, especially the Institute for Defense Analyses (IDA). The latter was a nonprofit consortium of twelve universities, including Columbia, which had been formed in 1955 to sponsor approved research projects requested by the military, especially the Army and the Navy.

In *February 1968*, a sit-in was staged by about 80 students in Dodge Hall to protest recruiting by the Dow Chemical Company.

Also in *February 1968*, construction began on the gymnasium in Morningside Park. A number of demonstrators, including some students, were arrested, but neither the Students for a Democratic Society (SDS) nor the Student Afro-American Society (SAS) was involved.

On *March 20*, a demonstration disrupted a speech by the New York City director of Selective Service, and a pie was thrown in his face.

A week later, on *March 27*, the SDS staged a demonstration in Low Library, directly challenging a presidential rule, and in consequence leaders of the group were placed on probation.

PROLOGUE

The University held a memorial service for Martin Luther King, Jr. in St. Paul's Chapel on *April 9*. The service was interrupted by Mark Rudd, a leader of the SDS. He seized the microphone in the chancel, denounced the proceedings as "a moral outrage against Dr. King's memory," and then, with a score of his followers, left the premises. No black students participated in the disruption.

The major uprising began on *Monday afternoon, April 23*, with a rally by the SDS at the Sundial located on College Walk (formerly 116th street) in the center of the Columbia campus, followed by an encounter at the gymnasium site, a sit-in in Hamilton Hall, and the taking of the dean of Columbia College, Harry Coleman, as a hostage.

Early on the morning of *April 24*, the black students evicted the white students from Hamilton Hall, after which a group of the white students broke into Low Library and seized the president's office. At 3 p.m. a long meeting of the College Faculty was held, ending in the adoption of a resolution whose most crucial provision stated, "we trust that police action will not be used." At about 10 p.m.., architecture students refused to leave Avery Hall, thus beginning an occupation of that building.

At approximately 2 a.m. on *Thursday, April 25*, Fayerweather Hall was seized by a group of students; at the outset most of them were graduate students.

After the Mathematics Building was taken over by a group of those who were occupying Low Library at about 1 a.m. on *Friday, April 26*, President Kirk called for police assistance. This request was withdrawn about two hours later as a result of protests from faculty who were part of what came to be called the Ad Hoc Faculty Group

(AHFG). At the same time the administration announced that the construction on the new gymnasium had been suspended.

On *Saturday, April 27*, the chairman of the Board of Trustees, William E. Petersen, speaking for the board as well as for himself, issued on the campus a hard-line, no compromise statement.

An unprecedented meeting of the faculties of all of the Columbia schools on Morningside Heights was held in the Law School auditorium on *Sunday morning, April 28*. A resolution supportive of the administration's efforts to end the crisis was adopted without any reference to possible police action. Approximately at the same time, the AHFG issued a resolution making a series of demands upon the administration and upon those occupying the buildings. This resolution came to be called the "bitter pill."

On *Monday, April 29*, President Kirk issued a response to the "bitter pill" that accepted a substantial portion of its demands. The Strike Committee of the SDS, speaking for those occupying the buildings, rejected outright the provisions of the faculty resolution.

At about 1:30 a.m. on *Tuesday, April 30*, the New York Police Department, at the request of the University, removed those occupying the campus buildings and made a large number of arrests. Later in the day a second meeting of the faculties on Morningside Heights was held in St. Paul's Chapel, at which an Executive Committee of the Faculty was created.

On *May 4*, this committee created a fact-finding commission whose report was issued in October. The commission is known as the Cox Commission, after its chairman, Archibald Cox, and is so cited in these pages.

PROLOGUE

On *Friday, May 17*, Mark Rudd and about 400 others seized a University-owned building near the campus. The building was an apartment structure that was being used for offices. Police removed and arrested the occupants in the early hours of the next morning.

In protest over the disciplining of SDS leaders, Hamilton Hall was seized on the afternoon of *Tuesday, May 21*. The police emptied Hamilton during the night and, after protesters subsequently damaged various buildings on the campus, the police cleared the campus.

On *Tuesday, June 4*, the Columbia University Commencement was held in the Cathedral of St. John the Divine.

CHAPTER ONE
INTRODUCTION

Yes, the time has come when I should write my reflections on the events at Columbia University in the spring of 1968. The time may be overdue, but my reasons for delay have been, for the most part, sound. I had many invitations, supported by the urgings of friends and acquaintances, to write my views immediately after the events, but I resisted them. A number of interviews were given, including a long session, live, with a group of students from the School of Journalism, which was telecast on Channel 13 in New York on May 3, 1968, three days after the first police action, and a live appearance on WNBC's program, Searchlight, on May 19. A paper was prepared and read (for me rather than by me, since I was ill on the appointed date) at a meeting of the Council of Graduate Schools in San Francisco on December 5, 1968, and in 1970 a shorter version was given as a talk to the Amherst Faculty Club, subsequently published in the *Amherst Alumni News*. (Copies or transcripts of these materials are in my files. From time to time in the pages that follow I shall refer to them.) But that is essentially the only record I have made of these events, until now.

My reluctance to write sooner was not primarily that I felt the need for gaining perspective. It came rather from a profound need to put the events behind me psychologically, to pull out of the acute depression that plagued me in the months after May 1968, and to get on with putting my life back together, preferably in a new location, by taking on a new set of challenges having nothing to do with Columbia. I knew during the crisis that the depression reaction was coming, though it was more severe and more prolonged than I anticipated. I came home one night, about 4 a.m., Friday, April 26, and told my wife, who as usual was up and waiting for me, that I was discouraged and very much afraid that there was going to be no conclusion to the situation without bringing in the police. (I gave my reasons, which I shall not go into at this point.) She, realist the she is, said to me, "If that happens, you know what it will mean?" I said, "Yes, it will mean that I shall have to resign." (For many months I made that statement to no one else in the Columbia environment.)

The depression I felt was real and persistent. All summer my wife, aided and supported by my son and daughter-in-law, whose love and unfailing support were something I shall never forget, planned again and again activities and diversions that ordinarily I would have taken great pleasure in. Knowing what they were trying to do, I would try to rise to the occasion, but I seemed never to have my heart in it, and the normal satisfactions escaped me. Perhaps this was weak, stupid, or perverse, but it was real and it was not deliberate.

The source of my feeling was not primarily sadness at an impending separation from Columbia, although it was impossible not to have some such sentiment. One cannot spend 18 years between the ages of 37 and 55, the center of one's most productive years, without feeling some hurt when the connection is about to be broken. I had been deeply involved in the institution, to the point, probably foolish,

INTRODUCTION

of rejecting a great many opportunities to move elsewhere. I had stayed partly because of a deep respect and indeed affection for many colleagues, but I had remained also out of a comparable respect for the past and the potential of a great university. My reaction did not derive from a feeling of failure, although again a little of that must have been involved, even if I felt, as I did, that the confrontation was, or became, unavoidable.

No, my depression came from the nightmarish experience of witnessing, of experiencing, what can properly be described as the disintegration of a great university, of learning, first-hand, that a university is an extraordinarily fragile institution. It is not fragile in the sense that it can easily go out of existence. No established institution, let alone one that has over two centuries of history, literally disappears; in name and form it is very nearly indestructible. The sort of disintegration to which I refer is the disruption of the fabric of trust and of tolerance that is at the heart of a college or university worthy of the name, and, with or consequent to that disruption, the demoralized departure from the institution of many of those who had made it what it was.

The fragility, in this sense, derives from the essential fact that the institution thrives on dissent. Heterodoxy is in its life's blood, but, if it is not to be poisoned, the dissent must be associated with a tolerance, not one that is indiscriminate, or one that permits intellectual dishonesty to go unchallenged, but one that insists that within the university there is no orthodoxy except intellectual integrity and a loyalty to the ideal of responsible dissent as essential to the mutual growth and accomplishment of the members of the institution. The fragile fabric of dissent is not normally threatened by the members having to choose between differing intellectual positions. That is routine and, in a healthy place, is done without rancor and without destruction of the ties of colleagueship. (From time to time such differences can degenerate into personal hostility, a situation that typically provides the material for academic novels and possibly explains why novels with an academic setting typically fall well short of greatness. The foibles and eccentricities that they focus upon are amusing but rarely profound. Such foibles, however, do not threaten the institution.)

What is threatening is a compelling pressure upon members to choose up sides concerning a matter that is outside the purview of the institution and that it cannot control even if its members should be in total agreement on it. Excepting the fairly rare case in which the matter at issue is perceived from within the university as a threat to the institution's survival, when a substantial unity may result, an extramural threat is almost inevitably disruptive.

Such matters typically are political; often they are associated with views concerning the legitimacy of war. This kind of threat appeared during World War I, when, especially before American involvement, to oppose such involvement risked being labeled "pro-German" and being dismissed from a faculty. It seemed about to appear during World War II, when, before Pearl Harbor, those with isolationist views, sympathizers with America First, were in some quarters suspected of being "disloyal." It was supremely evident during the Vietnam War, which, whatever additional factors one associates with the upheavals of the 1960s, was central to those disturbances and certainly to what occurred at Columbia. The intensity of feeling on other "issues," stated and implied, may have been more evident, but

INTRODUCTION

these would not likely have proved as explosive if it had not been for the war.

Such questions of war and peace are not readily amenable to the debating processes that universities are accustomed to. They call into question all sorts of qualities and personal inclinations that are not visible in the course of normal academic disputation. They are exogenous if not extraneous to the institution, and they can be accommodated only with difficulty and at risk to the fabric of tolerance. They threaten the university with disintegration. Especially within the faculty they produce virulent factionalism. They not only generate inter-factional hostility but more seriously threaten factional passion above loyalty to the institution.

It is easy to see and to say this from the perspective of 25 years. To experience it up close and for the first time is a shattering experience; the more so if one is in a position of formal responsibility. Hence, my disinclination to write about it at the time and my need to put the whole experience behind me. That I have done, but now I am almost provoked into writing by the appearance on various anniversaries of the Columbia uprisings of a series of maudlin, mawkish recollections and revisitations in the press and elsewhere. These trivialized a tragic occurrence and indicated that the authors and principals for the most part understood nothing of what had really happened and had learned nothing since. The anniversary observances confirmed my earlier decision to leave Columbia. I probably would have stayed, had I been asked, but I felt that the events of the crisis had surrounded me with such controversy that my capacity to induce healing and to stimulate reconstruction was severely limited.

REFLECTIONS ON THE COLUMBIA DISORDERS OF 1968

What I shall offer in the pages that follow are essentially reflections. I do not propose to write a history, a definitive account. I have neither the resources nor the inclination to do that. But I can write about how it looks to me, to the best of my ability how I felt and why I did what I did. (I do not intend to produce an *apologia pro vita sua*. Having relived those days hundreds of times in the past two and one-half decades, I have a fairly clear sense of where I may have been in error and of what I might have done that perhaps could have altered the outcome. I do not propose to suppress such self-criticism.) I can also here and there attempt to set the record straight and comment on some of those who have burst into print on the subject over the past two plus decades and who have, in my opinion, frequently fanciful, even fantastic, views of what went on and what was at stake.

I shall not present my reflections in chronological order. Perhaps if I had spent the 25th hour in each of the days of the crisis in keeping a diary, as was suggested afterwards by one of my well-meaning colleagues in the history department who, needless to say, was far from the center of the action, I might organize my thoughts in chronological fashion. But I kept no such record, because I couldn't, so I shall follow a topical outline. A number of reasonably accurate chronologies have been published and can be referred to even if the inferences drawn are in some instances unacceptable. (See, for example: Louis Lusky and Mary H. Lusky, "Columbia 1968: The Wound Unhealed," *Political Science Quarterly*, Vol. 84, No. 2, June, 1969, pp. 169–288, the result of a collaboration between a member of the Law School faculty and his daughter; *Crisis at Columbia: Report of the Fact-Finding Commission Appointed to Investigate the Disturbances at Columbia University in April and May 1968*, New

INTRODUCTION

York, Random House, 1968, cited as the Cox Commission Report; Jerry L. Avorn, et al., *Up Against the Ivy Wall: A History of the Columbia Crisis*, New York, Atheneum, 1969, by the staff of the undergraduate newspaper; George Keller, "Six Weeks That Shook Morningside," *Columbia College Today*, Vol. 15, No. 3, Spring, 1968, entire issue.)

I shall deal first with the question, why Columbia? The disturbances of 1968 and the immediately following years struck almost every university and college in the country, large or small, public or private, east or west, and they also broke out in universities over most of the globe. Why this geographic spread is another and separable question. The upheavals took somewhat different forms in different institutions and were of considerably varying intensity. These differences were rooted in the institutions' differing traditions and histories, in their peculiar problems and settings, and were reflected, therefore, in different local "issues" and grievances. What things were distinctive in the Columbia situation and why?

Second, I shall ask who were "the students" and what were their motives? These are not simple questions, not only because the evidence is scanty and frequently unreliable, but primarily because there was no homogeneous body of students nor a unified set of student purposes. One can easily forget that "the students" included many, the precise number impossible to estimate, who had no connection with Columbia. Many of the glib observations concerning the events of 1968 and their causes are specious just because they implicitly assume a homogeneous collection that can be labeled "the students." As it is analytically useless and misleading in political discourse to talk of "the people," so in this context is "the students" a

University's "back yard." An outbreak on Morningside Heights inevitably becomes national news, to an extent and with an intensity that would not occur if Columbia were located in New Haven, Princeton, or even Cambridge. This makes a Columbia problem more difficult to handle once it is "in the news," and it makes the University a particularly tempting target. The "local" media, including even the *New York Times* in comparatively quiet periods, are and were important to the University's functioning, but they are a part of the "big time" when a story goes national. The contribution of the media to the development of the crisis and to its "solution" is difficult to document with certainty, but that it was important is not debatable.

Finally, it may be useful to return to the very broad question: Why 1968? It is a question that is probably unanswerable, but it is also one that needs to be asked. The disturbances of the late 1960s and early 1970s were not confined to one campus or to one type of institution or even to the United States. They occurred in every sort of college and university in this country, in Britain, on the European continent, and essentially throughout much of the world outside of the Soviet Union and China. A phenomenon so widespread and so uniform in its general pattern, though its precipitating circumstances and associated local "issues" varied from place to place and from institution to institution, calls for some common explanation. Even if one attributes the widespread character of the disturbances to imitation, not a satisfying or highly persuasive explanation, one must still ask why. Answers have been offered by a wide variety of observers, from the local psychologizing reporter to the late Raymond Aron ("Student Rebellion: Vision of the Future or Echo from the

INTRODUCTION

Past?" *Political Science Quarterly*, Vol. 84. No. 2, June 1969), but no consensus has emerged. Perhaps, as with many major and complex causal questions in history, none will develop. Still, a discussion of any example of the phenomenon is not complete if it fails to ask why. I intend to raise the question and to attempt a speculative answer or two.

CHAPTER TWO
WHY COLUMBIA?

The Cox Commission was correct in its conclusion that "the University was deficient in the cement that binds an institution into a cohesive unit." (Cox, p. 194) It was also correct in many of its assertions concerning what was lacking in the "cement," although a number of these factors, allegedly peculiar to Columbia, were, in my judgment, present in the operation of most or all universities. (For example, the alleged unresponsiveness of the University to the needs of black students, the asserted preference of older faculty for autonomy as individuals to collective responsibility, the supposed indifference of the faculty to the noncurricular needs of students, and so on.) Many of the latter, however, were accentuated by circumstances peculiar to Columbia. These should be examined, even at the risk of repeating items that are discussed in the Cox Report and elsewhere. They are an essential part of the background and need to be reviewed in one location, which I shall do in this chapter, leaving some detailed discussions to later chapters.

Ever since the late 1930s, Nicholas Murray Butler's declining years, Columbia had been drifting, and in certain of its divisions, actually declining. The strong Butler heritage, which gave credibility to the appellation "Nicholas Miraculous," persisted in many forms, setting of these years the barons were the deans of the professional schools.

The power and substantial autonomy of the principal professional school deans on the Morningside campus were symbolized architecturally in the design and location of the new buildings that they built in the 1950s and 1960s. Mediocre in design at best, they showed no aesthetic respect for the elegant if run-down older McKim, Mead, and Whit structures and for the campus design that they reflected. The Law School, for example, referred to by local critics as "the toaster," for its vertical ribbing that resembled spaces for large slices of bread, included a block-long bridge over Amsterdam Avenue, which almost obscured St. Paul's Chapel. The latter is one of the real gems of the Columbia campus, but its beautiful brickwork and terra cotta are shouldered aside by the bridge, whose entrance to the campus proper thrusts itself between two of the older buildings.

The Engineering building, a huge brick, factory-like structure occupying what was the last open space at the north end of the campus, was appropriately referred to as the box that "the toaster" came in. Finally, the Business School, a tower that might have been at home somewhere in Midtown, was erected in the very center of the campus, behind but overshadowing Low Library, on a base formed by a long incomplete building dating from the early years on the Heights and known as University Hall. (University Hall, be it noted, contained, among other facilities, the hopelessly outmoded gymnasium and swimming pool.)

Buildings express values, purposes, and commitments, often unintentionally, but nonetheless accurately, and these spoke not only to the dominance of the professional schools, but also to the fragmentation of the University and especially the arts and sciences.

Disintegration in the years following World War II was also fostered by the invigorated movement to the suburbs. That movement, felt in all metropolitan areas, was on balance aggravated in New York and particularly in areas like Morningside Heights by the misguided retention of wartime rent control. The effects of that policy included an accentuated decline in the quality of building maintenance and the encouragement of the practice of cutting up apartments in order to put three, four, or more families in quarters previously occupied by one.

University policy itself encouraged abandonment of faculty residences on the Heights. Most critical in this connection was the decision taken in 1940 to merge Lincoln School with Horace Mann School and in 1946 turn the modern building of the combined school over to the city for use as a public school. Horace Mann had been run by Teachers College as a demonstration and experimental school. (The *New York Times*, February 19 and March 6, 1946, and May 2, 1948) Presumably Teachers College, an institution affiliated with Columbia University but having its own trustees, president, and faculty, concluded that the combined schools no longer fit into its program, were a financial drain on its resources, or for other reasons should not be continued. This decision precipitated a vigorous and prolonged but unsuccessful struggle.

In these interregnum years no one at the top level of the University proper seems to have recognized the stake that the University had in the continuance of these institutions of education. Reflection on the significance of school quality to personnel recruitment by the University generally might have clarified that and no vision of the University's needs or of where it should be heading. One example, of many that might be noted, is that he strenuously resisted the establishment of a central fund-raising program, despite Columbia's clear needs financially and in the face of the obvious fact that every other major university, from Harvard to Stanford, was engaged in serious efforts to raise capital. In the middle 1960s he was essentially tricked into launching a University drive by his then vice president, the late Lawrence H. Chamberlain, who in desperation used the opportunity of an address on a major University occasion to spell out Columbia's financial needs and to indicate what should be done to meet them. Kirk was not pleased, but he had either to accept the idea or repudiate his vice president. He chose the former, but he did not really throw himself into the effort, leaving most of the work to the deans, which, for the reasons already indicated, meant essentially the principal professional-school deans. Kirk's defenders could say with some degree of accuracy that in his years a good deal of money was raised, but they should also say that almost all of it was raised by and for the professional schools and without any University-wide plan. I recall hearing from an officer of a major foundation of an example of the absence of a central plan, who reported that, having received four or five proposals from different parts of Columbia, called the president to inquire what his priorities were among them. The answer, in effect if not so many words, was that he had no such priorities.

Kirk continued to "preside," a conception that was not visibly disastrous in the 1950s and early 1960s, but as times changed in the late 1960s it was increasingly inadequate, and the inadequacies became more and more widely apparent.

These things said, and before discussing some of the implications of this quick sketch, I should in fairness say that Grayson Kirk could be very charming. He was a sophisticated man, with cultured and discriminating tastes in food and especially wines. He is the only man I have ever known who was sure enough of his judgment and fearless enough of waiters and sommeliers to send a tasted bottle of wine back to the cellars. That takes a certain courage. A different and more impressive kind of courage was required for him to deal with a persistent stammer, which would appear without warning in a conversation or meeting. I never knew it to occur when he was reading a speech, though it may have, and I assume that it was a constant danger. In ordinary exchanges it must have been a frightful threat never to know when a humiliating stammer would manifest itself.

Kirk's presiding, reign-but-not-rule conception of the presidency included his acceptance of a very wide range of time-consuming positions outside the University. Something of this sort occurs to most university presidents, unless, as in the case of Harvard, there is a strong rule or precedent that the president does not assume outside responsibilities. In Kirk's case a number of these obligations were of a public, unremunerative and worthy character and in consequence would have been difficult to decline. But a substantial number were positions on corporate boards of directors, positions requiring regular time commitments and carrying with them substantial additions to income. Kirk once told Schuyler Wallace that he used his University salary chiefly to pay the income taxes on his outside earnings on corporate boards, a shocking revelation of how his time was spent and a most imprudent comment to a member of the faculty whose salary following a stormy but not seriously disorderly encounter over campus recruiting by the CIA. This occurred in November 1966, and the meeting with the president was characterized by Cox as "in the best tradition of university dialogue." Kirk also followed a practice that I had introduced when I was dean of the College, of meeting for informal, give-and-take exchanges in the dormitories. I made a practice of doing this at least once a semester in each of the five major dormitories. Kirk, beginning somewhat later, usually met the students in one dorm on two occasions each year. Like his other efforts along this line, however, they seem not to have been successful in eliminating the stereotype of the distant executive.

Kirk was not always so fortunate or so careful. The most conspicuous and even tragic example of this related to the report of the President's Committee on Student Life. This committee, established after a set of violent demonstrations in May 1965 that disrupted a Naval ROTC awards ceremony, was made up of equal numbers of students, faculty, and administrators. It was directed to "re-examine the existing University policies governing student rights and responsibilities." I was a member of the committee and I can certify that the group labored long and hard on the report that was submitted to the president in August 1967. By that time I had been made vice president and provost of the University, and I did not feel that I could formally "receive" or act on a report that I had helped to write, especially as there were parts of the report with which I did not agree, though I had signed the report, as had others who had their reservations. I explained my position to Kirk when the report was delivered to him.

President Kirk took no action on the report. I kept no record of the occasions when I urged him to act and to make the report public, but they were many. His only formal act was on September 25, 1967, when he issued a statement prohibiting picketing or demonstrations inside any University building. This had not been among the committee's recommendations, although it had debated the issue extensively, and the recommendation that it did make was delicately balanced in recognition of its controversial potential.

Kirk for months declined either to comment on the report or to release it, until he was forced to make it public when the University Student Council threatened to give its copy to the press. But he still declined to comment on any of its provisions, and he was quoted as saying that "For me to comment . . . would foreclose discussion about it on campus" and that "I would not want to say at this time in what spheres of University life the students should have a voice, because there has not been time to read the report carefully enough." This after seven months!

The most obvious result of this unfortunate sequence of events was that Kirk lost "control" of the issue concerning the report and its contents, at minimum in the eyes of those who had prepared the report, including faculty and administrators as well as students, and at maximum before a growing audience on the campus and eventually in the larger outside world, as the media commented on the Columbia crisis after the police action. In today's political parlance he lost "spin control." This situation was the more serious because Columbia not only had no professional public relations officer, but it also had no direct means for the president and others in the administration to communicate, by print or otherwise, with the campus, including both faculty and students.

As was the case in many universities in those days, the means of communication were in the hands of the student newspaper and the student radio station. The administration relied on conventional means of getting the word out, by memorandum, orally through departmental channels, and by an occasional press conference. The leaders of the SDS, on the other hand, showed great skill in using both the campus media and the increasingly important metropolitan and national channels. (See chapter 11.) On the campus, moreover, they had an impressive array of electronic equipment, walkie-talkies, bull phones, and the like, of which the University had nothing equivalent. (One wonders in such circumstances where the considerable amounts of money came from that produced such a communications armament.)

Although the University, as it has subsequently recognized, needed a channel of communication to the campus that was independent of student control, if only because judgments can differ on what it is important to report, it would be unfair to say that either the *Columbia Daily Spectator*, the student paper, or WKCR, the student-run FM station, abandoned all objectivity. I had no time in the days of the uprising to pay sustained attention to either, but reliable informants at the time and others writing after the events (Lusky and Lusky, p. 229) support my impressions. The weakness was that the University was not organized or equipped to handle a major public relations challenge (until, as it later developed, "the horse had been stolen from the barn").

WHY COLUMBIA?

The record shows, despite these deficiencies, that Kirk was not unaware of the problems presented by student unrest in the 1960s and of their sources. Nor was he completely a "hard-liner" in the face of their criticisms. On April 12, 1968, at the University of Virginia, he delivered a Founder's Day address in which he acutely analyzed the perilous state of the country, advocated in unequivocal terms the early end of our involvement in Vietnam, and described the "gap between the generations" as "wider . . . [and] more potentially dangerous" than at any time in our history. This was his speech, which he composed, as was his usual practice, without consulting anyone on the staff or faculty. It could have been important, yet it received no distribution on the campus. It was paid no attention there except by the local SDS, who recognized its challenge.

I never discussed this speech with Kirk, either before or after it was written, and I cannot help wondering what he intended it to accomplish at Columbia. Or did he see it simply as a proper academic observance of the 225th anniversary at Charlottesville, which it was, of course? But it might have been much more on Morningside Heights if it had been part of an effort to recapture the leadership of the University, seen as a step in reshaping the image of the University in the community, and most important, perhaps, used as a means of changing student and faculty perceptions of their president. Tragically, it was none of these.

Among the other vulnerabilities of Columbia and the consequent handicaps of Grayson Kirk was the person and position of the University treasurer, William Bloor, a devoted and in some ways extremely able University officer, but misguided in some of his activities and totally miscast in some of the functions that were attached to his position. As the officer responsible for investments, he quite properly reported to the Finance Committee of the Board of Trustees and not to the president. The latter was handicapped, however, by the dominant investment philosophy, inherited by Bloor, which was to place all or most of the University's endowment in real estate rather than in securities. Right or wrong, this policy had the effect that Columbia—unlike other major private institutions—completely missed the enormous rise in the stock market in the 1950s. (Harvard's endowment is reliably reported to have increased more in this period from equity investments than from all the capital gifts that it received.)

But the investment role of the treasurer was less serious for the operating vulnerabilities of Columbia and its president than the functions of the treasurer as de facto chief financial officer of the institution. In that capacity he managed all the residential real estate owned by the University on Morningside Heights. He was Columbia-as-landlord, and he single-handedly was more responsible for the University's bad relations with the local community, the origin of more of the justified complaints, of which there were many, than anyone else in the institution. He had no sense of public relations, to put the point gently, and he followed a rental policy, in managing the Morningside real estate, that not only gave tenants offense, but, more seriously, placed no value on the encouragement of facilities such as good grocery stores, decent restaurants, and repair shops that would contribute to the neighborhood and its quality of life. On the contrary, he followed a rental policy that drove such enterprises away; their number became smaller and smaller as the years went by, replaced by fast-food places, delicatessens, and other marginally helpful undertakings, ones geared to a transient and not to a settled residential population. His operating policies left no room for a planned rental loss on a retail establishment whose presence would contribute to the quality of life on the Heights. His practices, combined with a nonexistent public relations operation, left the way open for various self-designated "community leaders," such as the notorious Marie Runyon, whose public agendas appeared to be devoted to the community, but whose private purposes were in fact dominant and wholly self-serving. Marie Runyon rented an apartment in a building owned by the University on Amsterdam Avenue. Like most occupants of such buildings, she had no other connection with Columbia. She first became active when it was proposed that the site be used for a new building for the College of Pharmacy and the treasurer's office began to relocate tenants. Her visible agenda, the one reported in the *New York Times*, was to stop the University's encroachment on the surrounding area. Her hidden agenda was to protect an enterprise that she was reliably reported to operate, namely, subleasing rooms in her apartment. By renting rooms to graduate students or other individuals, she could reduce the net cost of her rent-controlled apartment to a minor amount, and the University managers could do nothing to stop her. (Apparently, Runyon made something of a career of attacking Columbia. She was pictured in an article in the *New York Times* on January 31, 1980, nearly 12 years after the crisis, with a caption under her photograph that read "Accuses the university of having 'a company-town syndrome.'")

For whatever reason, Kirk never succeeded in taking these landlord responsibilities away from the treasurer, if, as I think it was the case, he tried.

Bloor was not responsible, however, for the proposed gymnasium in Morningside Park, which became a central focus of the uprising in April 1968. That was a more complicated story, elements of which I shall deal with in later chapters.

Less serious for the University, in a way, but presenting an almost unmanageable obstacle to rational budgeting, was the refusal of the treasurer as de facto chief financial officer to supply the University management with an estimate of the endowment income for the coming year. I was responsible for making only one University academic budget, for 1968–69, and I was unable directly or through the president to get an estimate of the endowment income that could be expected. The treasurer gave the impression that this was a figure to which the University administration was not entitled.

On these several counts, the University treasurer was a part of the vulnerability of the institution and of its president. They were aggravated, as was the University's financial position, by the failure to exploit Columbia's bicentennial in 1954 by mounting a substantial capital drive. The anniversary was observed with impressive conferences, convocations, awarding of honorary degrees, and publication of proceedings, as at the anniversaries of other "colonial" colleges, but, unlike the others, Columbia made no effort to raise new endowment funds. This was especially unfortunate, since a number of tenured professorships had been established, especially in the School of International Affairs, on "soft" money. The Ford Foundation, especially, in these years was making expendable grants to encourage research and training in international fields. Some conservatively managed universities insisted successfully that the creation of professorships required gifts large enough to endow them. Columbia did not, and as grant policy began to shift in the 1960s, these salaries had to be supported by the general funds of the University, which had not been proportionately augmented.

Columbia salaries were not holding up competitively in the 1960s. For this and other reasons, the faculty, especially in the arts and sciences, was suffering serious losses, with a few conspicuous departmental exceptions. Cox was correct in reporting such losses (Cox, pp. 41ff) although he was misinformed in some instances about which departments were especially hard hit. But the particulars were less important in any event than the underlying fact that faculty morale was low. It was reflected in the declining national ratings of the graduate programs in the arts and sciences, and the latter contributed to producing confirming incidents on the national scene. For example, in April 1967 the Ford Foundation announced a grant program in support of doctoral studies in the arts and sciences at ten major universities. The implication of the announcement, of course, was that these were THE ten universities, and Columbia was not among them.

Cox (p. 44) correctly reports that "Many of the faculty were both surprised and upset." He also quotes McGeorge Bundy, president of the Ford Foundation, as saying that Columbia "lacked the motivation for reform."

I do not know the grounds for this statement, but I do know that, as dean of Columbia College, I was not only upset. I was horrified and angry. I at once arranged to have lunch with F. Champion Ward, vice president of the Foundation and in whose area this program fell. I not only expressed my distress but asked how they could have taken an action like this, which placed the prestige of the Foundation behind a rating that excluded Columbia from the ranks of the top ten universities in the country. I spoke as a friend, and he answered as one. He was apologetic and insisted that he had had no intention that such an inference concerning Columbia should be drawn. He then told me that they had talked with the then dean of the Graduate Faculties at Columbia, Ralph Halford, about the proposed program, and these conversations had led them to the conclusion that Columbia was not interested.

In the circumstances, my horror and dismay shifted from the Foundation to the Columbia campus. Halford was one of a triumvirate composed of Jacques Barzun, the dean of faculties and provost, Lawrence Chamberlain, the vice president, and Halford—sometimes augmented by Stanley Salmen, a coordinator of University planning. This group, which referred to itself as the Cabinet, was in effect managing the University. The presidency was practically in commission. The horror to me was that apparently neither this group nor anyone in it knew or recognized that it was imperative that Columbia be in and interested in any such program, not necessarily for financial reasons, important though those were, but because the morale and public relations consequences of not being in the selected group would be negative in the extreme. I registered my protests with Halford and Chamberlain, but of course it was too late to repair the damage.

Jacques Barzun was a key figure throughout these years of decline, both symptom and source of much that was wrong. Made dean of the Graduate Faculties in 1955 and raised to the new position of dean of faculties and provost in 1958, he was central to the central administration of the University until his resignation in 1967. He was not widely respected by the faculty and was mistrusted by some, including some members of the Board of Trustees who blocked his designation as a vice president of the University.

Barzun was given to sweeping and sometimes perceptive observations on the state of higher education, but he gave no leadership to the solution of substantive educational problems at Columbia. Despite faculty losses and the decline in the ratings of graduate programs, I have no evidence that he made any effort to plan and press for strengthening steps. Nor, either as dean or as provost, did he intervene or induce the president to intervene in an attempt to keep important members of the faculty whom other institutions were attempting to woo away. He and Kirk almost invariably left it up to the department chairmen, sometimes assisted by the Dean of the Graduate Faculties, to attempt to dissuade people from accepting competing offers or to participate in bargaining with people whom the departments were attempting to attract. Repeatedly people left the faculty with the feeling that, outside their departments, no one at Columbia cared whether they left or stayed.

I knew these things as a member of the faculty and as a department chairman. When I became dean of the College in 1963, I determined to try to correct them, although matters of this sort did not fall formally within my ambiguous mandate. Through my connections in the faculty I usually heard when someone of importance was being tempted to leave, and I made a practice of talking to the individual, sometimes also to his chairman, to inquire about what might induce him to stay and, most important, to make it clear that at least the dean of the College wanted him to stay. On occasion I intervened not only with the graduate dean or with Barzun, but also with the president. I was not always successful, but I know that I did prevent some departures and, where I failed, I had reason to believe that the individual left with a better taste in his mouth than if I had not acted. I did some good, but the dean of the College could not, in this kind of activity, really replace the top administration of the University.

Barzun was enamored of procedural reforms. Some of these were good and useful, but a number of them seemed to me to illustrate perfectly John Gardiner's perceptive observation that the last act of a dying organization is to issue a new and revised edition of the rule book. Thus he introduced an elaborate and complicated system for numbering courses and for cross-listing them in different parts of the arts and sciences—the College, the Graduate Faculties, the School of General Studies (GS), and so on. Presumably this was a device for reducing the number of courses, a worthy objective, but it was circuitous and ineffectual. In the College it often had the effect of diluting the undergraduate experience, especially when day students in the School of General Studies were registered alongside College students.

Barzun professed a dedication to the College, of which he was an alumnus, but his handling of the School of General Studies illustrates his failure to see, or to acknowledge, the implications of his policies. General Studies grew out of Extension, a familiar adjunct to many universities. As time went on, moreover, there was very good reason for having a school of adult or continuing education, primarily in evening programs, one that could award degrees as well as sponsor special nondegree programs. Under Barzun's sponsorship, however, the School began to admit students of the same age as those admitted to the College and to Barnard, and to schedule a full program of daytime courses leading to an undergraduate degree. The result was that students began to turn up in the School whom the College had declined to admit; these students then tried to transfer into the College and were offended when they were turned down. As dean of the College I finally put an end to this back-door admissions practice by writing a long and detailed protest to the president, spelling out the problem and proposing that the minimum age for admission to the School of General Studies be raised to twenty. When this was done, the dean of the School, my friend from college days, the late Clifford Lee Lord, resigned, feeling justifiably that he had been betrayed. (He subsequently devoted his considerable talents to Hofstra University, of which he became president.)

Among Barzun's "reforms" was the introduction of an ad hoc committee system for reviewing and making recommendations concerning departmental proposals for granting tenure to members of the faculty. Basically the idea was a good one. Leaving such decisions almost entirely up to the departments was not good for the establishment and maintenance of standards or for preventing the perpetuation of mediocrity. The Barzun system, however, differed in major respects from that employed in the Faculty of Arts and Sciences at Harvard. In the first place, the Columbia system relied entirely on members of its own faculty from outside the nominating department, whereas the members of the Harvard ad hoc committees were almost always outsiders in the same field as the candidate. Second and more important, no one from the central administration attended the meetings of the committees, which reported their recommendations in writing to the provost. At Harvard, on the other hand, the president of the University and the dean of the Faculty of

Arts and Sciences met with and presided at the ad hoc committee meetings, usually spending an entire half day in such sessions, which took no formal votes and made no written report. (When I became provost, the dean of the Graduate Faculties and I agreed that, in order to protect the integrity of the system, to introduce into it some uniformity of criteria, and to have it contribute significantly to our information, he or I or both of us would attend all ad hoc committee meetings.)

The ad hoc system at Columbia thus not only did nothing to bridge the gap between the president and members of the faculty but also it contributed to a feeling of distance from the central administration, of nonparticipation. (This feeling undoubtedly was greater among the fairly numerous Columbia faculty members who knew the Harvard practice from service on such committees in Cambridge.) The point is important because commentary on the 1968 crisis underscores the weakness of structures for faculty participation in university decision making and in some cases inaccurately alleges that no such mechanisms existed.

A mechanism for faculty participation in University policy did exist. It was weak, and its weakness and the reasons therefore were pivotal in the handling and the aftermath of the 1968 crisis. This body was the University Council, which Cox (Cox, p. 34) dismisses, saying that there was "no university senate or similar body to represent the faculties as a whole" and that "The University Council is a small body that concerns itself with formal programs of study and the requirements for higher degrees."

A senate by another name can still function as a senate, and the appropriate size for such a body is not prescribed by enduring custom.

WHY COLUMBIA?

The University Council, whose origins lay decades in the past, had come to confine its activities to the formalities that Cox lists, but it was not always so. I do not know what it did in the Butler days, but I recall that it operated as a constructive and useful forum for discussing the threat posed in the early 1950s by Senator Joseph McCarthy. It was not poorly composed for such purposes. In 1968 it was comprised of forty elected faculty, two from each of the several schools, the nineteen deans of those schools as members ex officio, plus the president of the University and a handful of other University officers. It was thus in substantial measure a faculty body whose members were elected by their colleagues.

The University Council played no role whatsoever in the management of the 1968 crisis. It had been allowed to atrophy, so that perhaps it could not have made a useful contribution, but it was not called upon. I thought it should have been convened, and I still think so. But President Kirk adamantly refused to have it meet. Over and over again I urged him to convene the Council so that, if distasteful decisions had to be taken, a properly constituted body with a substantial faculty representation from the whole University could participate and could be seen to have participated. He firmly refused.

Those refusals had a number of consequences, for Kirk and for the University. They included the de facto creation of a large and officially unempowered faculty body, the Faculties of the University on Morningside Heights, which met in the Law School auditorium on Sunday, April 28, and adopted a generally supportive resolution and which met a second time in the Chapel on Tuesday afternoon, April 30, and adopted a resolution creating an Executive Committee of the Faculty, which thenceforward effectively subordinated the presidency on matters growing out of the crisis and of the aftermath of the first police action. The consequences also included the emergence of self-appointed faculty aggregations such as the Ad Hoc Faculty Group, which attempted to take over the management of the crisis and to determine policy in the wake of the police action.

These matters I shall discuss further in later chapters. Here the important points are why the University Council had been allowed to atrophy and why Kirk was determined not to convene it.

I, as provost, felt that I had a stake in the Council. To strengthen it and to help bridge the gulf between faculty and administration, in the fall of 1967 I had discussed in the Council and with the chairmen of departments in the arts and sciences the problems of the University budget and other matters in which I or members of these groups were interested. Perhaps it was to these efforts that Cox referred when he said, "About a year ago the Administration gave evidence of its desire to begin to evolve a system of greater participation, but no actual changes were accomplished." (Cox, p. 34)

As one who for many years was a member of the Council, I was well aware that for both Kirk and Barzun it was regarded as no more than a formal ratifying body and a nuisance rather than a means of consultation and advice. On occasion, however, the formal powers of the Council and its ratifying functions could produce significant, if sometimes unexpected, results. A major case of this type occurred about 1959, when the president and Barzun proposed, on behalf of Dean Courtney Brown of the Business School, that the Faculty of the Graduate School of Business be empowered to award the Ph.D. degree. They did not reckon with the late Lawton P. G. Peckham, who had succeeded Barzun as dean of the Graduate Faculties and ex officio a member of the University Council.

Parker Peckham was a distinguished scholar in old French and an effective administrator who had been called upon more than once by the University to assume temporarily the chairmanship of a department, other than his own, whose members could not agree on one of their own number or on anything else. He was a civilized gentleman, superficially mild in manner, not bold but strong, courageous, and a man of conviction. Dean Peckham eloquently opposed the Business School proposal, arguing quite properly that the degree of doctor of philosophy is an arts and sciences and not a professional degree. He suggested, with the support of members from his faculties, that if the Business School wished to award a doctoral degree, as they well might, they could propose a professional doctorate, such a doctor of business administration. The result was that the Brown-Barzun-Kirk proposal was soundly defeated.

Neither Barzun nor Kirk was one to take a defeat gracefully or readily to forget opposition that they presumably regarded as insubordination. They did not revive the Brown proposal, but about a year later it was announced that Peckham was resigning as dean of the Graduate Faculties in order to return to teaching. Those who knew Peckham, as I did, knew that this was not true and that Peckham had been fired by Kirk on Barzun's initiative. Another who knew the truth was the late Marjorie Nicholson, distinguished scholar and for years the strong chairman of the impressive Department of English, one who had convictions and the courage thereof. Professor Nicholson went to Kirk to query and to protest the dismissal of Peckham, and,

CHAPTER THREE

"THE STUDENTS"— WHO WERE THEY?

"The students" was the term that the media (and others) used to designate those who were occupying the campus buildings or were otherwise participating in the activities that began on the afternoon of April 23, but it did not designate a homogeneous population; rather it included a diverse, at times extremely diverse, collection of individuals who were on the campus and in the buildings for a wide variety of reasons.

To be sure, a sizable majority of those in the buildings apparently were connected with Columbia University ("apparently" because the precise fractions are impossible to determine, given the circumstances, and must be estimated from such sources as the police arraignment reports and from the observations of newspaper reporters). Of these a majority, possibly most, of the occupants were enrolled in Columbia College. Some, however, were from Barnard College, and some were from the School of General Studies. Those in Fayerweather Hall were mostly graduate students from the arts and sciences departments, and of course Avery Hall was held by students in the School of Architecture.

The roster of Columbia participants also contained a considerable number of College students [the "Majority Coalition"] who opposed the building occupiers and who, as the days went by, were increasingly disposed to take direct action. Dean Harry Coleman and others were active and effective in dissuading these members of the Majority Coalition from any such move although this group probably did represent a majority of Columbia students, but not in an organized way. Only one prospect seemed uglier than physical conflict between groups of students, namely, a wave of sympathetic violence from residents of Harlem. Student against student was not a remote possibility, and in fact there were some scuffles around Low Library that were restrained only because alert members of the faculty intervened. Feelings ran high. As A. M. Rosenthal of the *New York Times* reported, there was "plain, almost tangible hatred between some of the students opposing the demonstrations and some of them supporting . . . [those] barricaded in the buildings." (May 1, 1968)

"The students" also included people from colleges throughout New York City and the metropolitan region. Until the report of the Cox Commission came out, I had not realized that on the afternoon of April 23, when Hamilton Hall was first seized, Mark Rudd of the SDS and Ray Brown of the SAS issued a call for assistance from various outside groups. Nor was the New York area or even the Northeast the only source of participants. Tom Hayden, SDS organizer from the University of Michigan, was on the campus soon after the troubles began, apparently spending most of his time in President Kirk's office in Low Library. Hayden was reported, however, to have been one of the party who on Thursday night, April 25, took over the Mathematics Building. (*New York Times*, April 27, 1968) Hayden, of course, later married and was divorced by Jane

"THE STUDENTS"—WHO WERE THEY?

Fonda and has been pursuing a modest political career in Southern California. (Where else?)

As the days went by and the demonstration became a major media event, attention from other luminaries was bound to come. Most of them did not stay, but, like Rap Brown, Stokely Carmichael, and others, made token appearances, long enough to face the forest of cameras and to make a statement to reporters.

From among these "outsiders" I probably should not omit some old socialists such as the late Dwight Macdonald, who, like certain members of the Columbia faculty, saw in the uprising at Columbia the development of the revolution that they had missed in their youths. According to William L. O'Neill:

> Though Macdonald was a very old leftist, the Columbia rising thrilled him as much as any undergraduate. The rebels thought themselves to be creating a new order. Macdonald was excited by memories of an older one. To him the occupied Mathematics Building was "the Smolny Institute of the revolution, the ultra-Left SDS stronghold . . . while Fayerweather was the Menshevik center"—that is, it favored a compromise settlement.

O'Neill quotes Macdonald as writing afterward, "I've never been in or even near a revolution before. I guess I like them. There was an atmosphere of exhilaration, excitement—pleasant, friendly, almost joyous excitement. Everybody was talking to everybody those days, one sign of a revolution." And he suggests that Macdonald might have added that it is also one sign of a disaster.

To Macdonald's confident assertion that students learned more in those six days than in years of classes, O'Neill comments:

> This observation was unfailingly made after every campus protest. But while doubtlessly true, it was

> certainly irrelevant. What they learned had nothing to do with what universities were designed to teach, and was accomplished at the expense of what the university did best.
>
> The university was hurt in ways that would not be fully known for years. . . . That so experienced a man as Dwight Macdonald could be swept along by them [the rebels] was, perhaps, only a further sign of how advanced national pathology had become. (William L. O'Neill, *Coming Apart: An Informal History of America in the 1960's*, p. 91)

Macdonald continued his part in the ordeal by speaking at the mock commencement, which took place on Low Plaza on June 4. According to press reports, he praised the "protesting students" but was "hissed when he said that if they looked upon the university merely as a tool for revolution," they would destroy it and "stimulate the already oppressive standards" of the nation. (*New York Times*, June 5, 1968)

Diversity, but not racial diversity, characterized the groups occupying the buildings. On the night of April 23, one building, Hamilton Hall, became the exclusive domain of black students (and temporarily some outsiders). Almost all of the occupants of the other four buildings, however, were white. Between the SDS and the SAS a certain amount of arm's-length cooperation existed during the demonstrations, but it affected only the leadership and them not very intimately. SDS was a white organization. Its leadership, most conspicuously Mark Rudd, did not mix well with black students and appeared to dislike them. In the incidents that occurred in the year or so prior to the explosion in April 1968, moreover, individual black students were occasionally but rarely involved. The two groups generally had different stakes in the University.

"THE STUDENTS"—WHO WERE THEY?

If the affiliations of "the students" were varied, their purposes and objectives were even more so. For those with Columbia affiliations, the material discussed in chapter 2 should indicate the sources of local dissatisfactions. These could be activated by the events beginning on April 23 even if they were not articulated in the "demands" that were made conspicuous at that time. The latter, about which more will be said in later pages, were stated by the SDS leadership and, during the occupation, served as a sort of rallying point for the disparate groups, a kind of least common denominator of stated objectives. The park gymnasium, discovered late by the SDS, drew the SAS into the picture and made a kind of policy bridge between the two groups and incidentally caused alarm in City Hall. The attack on the Institute for Defense Analyses was a surrogate for an attack on the military and the Vietnam War, while serving as a basis for convicting the University authorities of "complicity" in the war. And amnesty, the third highly visible demand, appealed to all who might be threatened with the costs of their actions. The leaders of the SDS were sensitive about the opportunism of their demands. When Mark Rudd was asked what his program was, he shouted back, "I don't have a program. I have a vision of a better world than yours, you mother-fucker." (*New York Times*, June 10, 1968)

The fissures that were covered by these "demands" began to appear almost immediately after the "bust" on April 30. A substantial segment of the rebellious students split off early from the SDS leadership. They were essentially a group of non-violent liberals whose interest was primarily in reforming University procedures and organization. They called themselves Students for a Restructured University.

Graduate students in a whole series of departments met with the faculty and, with the aid of pliant faculty sympathizers, adopted a range of consultative devices and rights of student participation as well as modifications of some degree requirements. (This last was a common result of disturbances on many campuses in the 1960s. Grade inflation and abolition of requirements seemed to be an almost universal consequence of the "troubles," although in most places these changes were fashionable in particular departments, mostly in the "softer" disciplines.) Some of these changes made sense and some were long overdue, but the unseemly haste with which many of them were embraced did not inspire confidence in the integrity or the wisdom of the faculty involved.

In Architecture the students got a hearing from the Dean and the faculty, many of whom were highly sympathetic, and with good reason.

Students in the School of General Studies (GS), or more accurately their self-designated representatives, came out with a series of their parochial demands, including the right to receive the B.A. degree rather than the B.S. This latter was a matter of dispute with the College and a hangover from the days when GS threatened to become a kind of low-quality rival of the College. The College faculty felt that the distinctive and demanding curriculum that it offered deserved a distinctive B.A. degree, while students and some faculty in GS thought that the B.S. degree made them second-class citizens. (The GS forces won that one after April 1968.)

These comments indicate the persisting diversity of participants and their purposes. They do not account, however, for that substantial but unknown number of students who were swept up in the emotional

"THE STUDENTS"—WHO WERE THEY?

atmosphere, which at times took on an almost carnival feeling. These could be participants without any focused purposes and totally without political motivation. For many on many campuses, as O'Neill rather harshly suggests, "Defying authority in a good cause was fun. . . . It was a mixture of living theater, cowboys and Indians, the Russian Revolution, and nursery school." (O'Neill, *Coming Apart*, p. 291) The incongruous carnival-like atmosphere reached a kind of climax in Fayerweather one afternoon during the occupation when a young couple was married there by the Reverend William Starr, Episcopal counselor to Protestant students. (A beneficent fate would have spared the University the curse of having him and his colleagues in the Chaplain's office assigned by their denominations to the campus.) The weird atmosphere is also illustrated by the sick fantasy, purporting to be the story of the uprising, published after the event as *The Strawberry Statement: Notes of a College Revolutionary*, by James S. Kunen, whose revolutionary ardor was rewarded by a profitable book, a moderately successful movie, and a job with *People* magazine.

As for the purposes and objectives of outsiders like Tom Hayden, who knows? Irving Howe suggested nearly 15 years later (*New York Times Magazine*, September 19, 1982) that these were by no means clear even after the events. Hayden stated after 1968 that "Columbia offered a new tactical stage in the resistance. . . . From the overnight occupation of buildings to permanent occupation, from the mill-in to the creation of revolutionary committees, from symbolic civil disobedience to barricaded resistance." To Howe "such statements must seem delusionary."

somewhat exaggerates the degree and character of the functioning organization, but in essence it is correct.

The Steering Committee was pivotal in all that followed over the next six days. It was dominated by a small group of SDS leaders, and they in turn were significantly influenced if not controlled by a small group of dedicated revolutionaries "whose object," in Cox's words, "was to subvert and destroy the university as a corrupt pillar of an evil society." (Cox, p. 58) That may seem to be a wildly extreme, even hallucinatory statement, but it is correct. Subsequent events in themselves go a long way to corroborate it. It was one of this group, Ted Gold, who in the summer of 1970 was among those killed when a bomb-making operation in the Wilkerson house in Greenwich Village blew up. And some years later, in the Brinks hold-up and murder in Rockland County, one of those arrested, convicted, and sentenced to a long prison term was David Gilbert, who had graduated from the College in 1966.

It is hard to make those statements, especially to recall the fate of David Gilbert. I had known him as an undergraduate. He was perhaps disturbed in some measure, but he was a bright, attractive, and quite likable young man. I knew that he was leftist in his politics, but that in itself was not a reason for concern. To have radical views, especially as an undergraduate, is not unhealthy. With Gilbert it had gone further than I realized. I shall never forget meeting him on the campus early in the morning of April 24. He was running toward Low Library. I called to him, "David! Stop! You've done enough." He laughed at me somewhat hysterically and ran on. I never saw him again.

"THE STUDENTS"—WHO WERE THEY?

The total lack of scruple among the members of this revolutionary clique is illustrated by the complete absence of contrition or any sense of regret for damage to the University after the worst of the uprising was over. Six weeks after the first police action, Lewis Cole, one of their leaders, was quoted as saying, "I would say our ends did justify the means—they are the only means allowable to us." (*New York Times*, June 10, 1968) It is also worth noting, perhaps, that when the police bust came on April 30, the SDS leadership clique were not in the buildings. Mark Rudd, for example, was arrested on two later occasions, but, forewarned on April 30, he and his colleagues were not on the campus. And as Allan Silver, a member of the Sociology Department, who thought he was being a mediator when in fact he was serving the purposes of this extreme group, eventually concluded, "Their moral arrogance is incredible." (*Ibid.*)

To return to the Steering Committee, it is accurate to say that it dominated, though it did not wholly control, the occupation. Its members succeeded in limiting the communications that reached the "communes," as the groups of occupiers were called, and in conveying instructions and information to them. This was true, at least, of four of the buildings. Hamilton Hall had its own organization and chose its own course. The visible role of the Steering Committee was to state the responses of the demonstrators to efforts by or on behalf of the University administration to reach an acceptable and peaceful settlement of the occupation. Its actual and intended role, however, was to force a confrontation with the University administration, to provoke a police action and, in consequence, to induce a radicalization of the campus.

REFLECTIONS ON THE COLUMBIA DISORDERS OF 1968

The relations between the communes and the Steering Committee apparently were not smooth. Reports reaching the University administration at the time, and reported to the public after the events, indicated that the disputes focused on different views of means-end morality, the revolutionaries viewing such concerns with contempt, though not always expressing their differences in those terms, and those who came to be referred to as "the liberals" being genuinely disturbed, if ineffectually, by the prospect that a defensible substantive case would be corrupted by an indifference to methods. This group bore some resemblance to the students at Duke with whom Douglas Knight had to deal as president. Speaking of the contrast with those on other campuses, he says of his students, "Even in their times of vigorous protest, they were a surprisingly polite and civilized group." (Knight, *Street of Dreams*, p. 119) In particular, the liberals at Columbia were ready to compromise on the demand for amnesty for all the demonstrators. Many of them were ready to accept some form of due process and uniform punishment for all participants. In fact, one commune, the group in Fayerweather, it later transpired, proposed such a formula late in the occupation. It was turned down by the Steering Committee without being referred to any of the other groups. The committee apparently was determined not to let the "liberal" view of amnesty affect strike tactics. (Hays, *Political Science Quarterly*, p. 321)

The problem for the administration, clearer by hindsight than it was in the midst of the week's turmoil, was to reach past this dominant group in the Steering Committee to the "liberals" and other less intransigent elements in the buildings. It was clear that there would be no negotiation with the strike leadership, as I found out when, responding on Thursday afternoon to what turned out to be a spurious request from the group in Low Library, I was peremptorily rejected, as I had been when I made an offer to meet with them on Tuesday afternoon.

In this effort we were completely unsuccessful, as subsequent events demonstrated. We were not aided by various self-appointed, though for the most part well-meaning members of the faculty, who entered the buildings or talked with occupants from the outside and brought back wisps of what they regarded as encouraging information. They were just wisps, and when these discussions were with members of the Steering Committee, as some of them apparently were, the emissaries' apparent respect for the Steering Committee could only have had the effect of enhancing the status of the committee members in the eyes of the other demonstrators. Nor were our efforts materially advanced by members of the faculty, whom we encouraged to reach into the communes because we had confidence in them and they appeared to be trusted by the rank and file of the demonstrators. With none of the five groups were we able to establish any effective communication.

As it gradually became apparent to me that we were not going to be able to reach past the radical minority that dominated the Steering Committee, I was forced to the reluctant conclusion that a confrontation was unavoidable. (Out of this conclusion I drew the title of the paper that I submitted but, because of illness, did not read to the Council of Graduate Schools at their San Francisco meeting on December 5, 1968: "The Dilemmas of an Unavoidable Confrontation.")

We continued to work toward another outcome, right through Monday, April 29, and the complexities of the administration's response to the so-called "bitter pill" resolution of the Ad Hoc Faculty Group, of which more in a later chapter. But it gradually became apparent to me that we were not going to succeed, even if we were to grant complete amnesty to all participants, which I knew President Kirk would not accept and which I was sure a majority of the trustees would oppose. When, exactly, I reached this conclusion, I do not know, but I think it was late Friday night. I was talking with my close friend and respected colleague, the late Herbert Deane, in the ground-floor corridor of Low Library, outside of the rooms we were using as offices. I confessed my apprehension to him and, for the first and only time during the whole episode, I broke down. He could not disagree, but he gave me comfort, which I shall never forget. And that night, or more correctly early the next morning, a few hours before dawn, when I returned to our apartment, where my wife, as always, was waiting up for me, I told her, in our brief conversation before I snatched some sleep, that I feared we would have to call in the police. As I reported in my introductory chapter, we agreed then that if my fears were confirmed, I would have to resign from my position and from Columbia.

The role of the extremists on the Steering Committee was succinctly summarized by James A. Wechsler, perhaps a suspect witness since he was a loyal Columbia alumnus. Writing in the *New York Post*, he observed that "the basic challenge [to the University] came from those who cherished conflict at any price, and held strategic command posts in the occupied territory." (April 30, 1968) Indications of the indifference to means kept coming up. On the night of May 21, the second occupation of Hamilton Hall, fire broke out in the office of Professor Orest Ranum on the sixth floor, and two file drawers of research notes were destroyed by fire and water. No other office in the building was broken into, and no other fires were set. Ranum had been notably critical, orally and in writing, of the first building occupations. A member of the Steering Committee was quoted on the day after the incident as saying, "It's no secret that he doesn't like us and that we don't like him." (*New York Times*, May 23, 1968) Members of the Committee later denied responsibility for the fire.

The potential of this clique of extremists for disruptive violence was the prime consideration in the decision in May to hold the University Commencement in the Cathedral of St. John the Divine, the rain location, rather than outdoors on Low Plaza, its usual location. We were criticized, later, for timidity, for "not daring to grasp the opportunity to let the SDS put its disruptive tactics on view." (Lusky and Lusky, p. 271) On the other side, we were questioned by the press when the decision was announced on the likelihood of an attempt to disrupt the ceremony. (*New York Times*, May 17, 1968)

One exchange went considerably beyond a query. Sometime after the announcement of the Cathedral location I was visited in my office by Archibald Cox, chairman of the Commission of Inquiry, who said he wanted me to go to President Kirk and propose the cancellation of Commencement. "If you attempt to hold it, even in the Cathedral, blood will run in the streets of this neighborhood." I declined his request, saying that in my judgment it was imperative that Columbia hold its Commencement, that he could go to President Kirk with his proposal if he wanted to, and that in the event that Kirk accepted it, I would resign immediately. As far as I know, he never went to Kirk.

At the time I was puzzled by his alarm. Years later, in a personal conversation, Cox told me that the challenge to the Columbia administration was the most difficult he knew of, because we were up against a group of real revolutionaries. He indicated that he had become aware of their fanaticism through informal contact that he had been able to establish with them even though they had refused to appear before the Cox Commission. That contact apparently had persuaded him that we should not risk a commencement ceremony.

Cox was not the only worried observer. I was visited at least half a dozen times by the late Geroid T. Robinson, professor of Russian history, who had made it his business to know every nook and corner of the Cathedral. On each visit he would identify one or more of these hiding places and express doubt that the police would be able to clear and control these spots at the time of the ceremony.

Robinson's anxiety was not entirely fanciful, and he was not the only Columbia person who was fearful. The late Richard Hofstadter, the distinguished historian who had been asked to make the commencement address when it was decided that the president should in prudence abandon the tradition of his giving it, came to me a week or so before the ceremony and said that he thought he should pull out of his agreement to give the address. When I questioned him on his reasons, he said that he had no worry about preparing it but was fearful of what might happen when he delivered it. He was, he said, a physical coward. That was something I did not believe and said so. I still do not believe it. People who are indeed cowards do not confess to being so. I expressed sympathy and urged Hofstadter, who was a

"THE STUDENTS"—WHO WERE THEY?

good friend, to get out of town, to prepare the speech at his cottage on Cape Cod and give himself the perspective afforded by distance. He did that. He gave without incident a brilliantly effective address, but his anxiety testifies to the general level of apprehension in the University community.

A word or two more needs to be said about the black students, how they conducted themselves, how critical they were early in the occupation to a possible solution to the whole problem, and what my personal relations were with them as a group.

Although some divisions existed among the black students, in general they were highly unified and remarkably disciplined. To be sure, they did not testify before the Cox Commission, although a handful of black students did appear at an early stage in the hearings and denounced the Commission for a number of alleged deficiencies, including its having no member from the Harlem community. This seems to me more a mark of the distance that the group generally maintained in relation to others in the University than a spirited challenge. In any event it does not alter the fact of their dignified and disciplined conduct through the whole affair. When the police action occurred on April 30, the black students exited from Hamilton Hall without resistance and to a man insisted on being arrested. It is also the case that during the first two days of the occupation we received credible reports that some of the occupants of Hamilton Hall had guns. No proof of this ever was found, and I am convinced that if the reports were true, it was outsiders—of whom there were some in Hamilton early in the occupation—and not Columbia students who were the offenders. (These reports did restrain us from attempting to force the release of Dean Coleman, who was held hostage for the first two days.)

As the Cox Commission correctly reports (Cox, pp. 111ff and 145ff), for the first two days the University administration concentrated its efforts on trying to reach an agreement with the black students in Hamilton Hall. For various reasons, some of which I do not and cannot know, these were unsuccessful. (I shall discuss some that I do know about in later chapters.) Cox is probably correct in saying that if they had succeeded, they would have been the key to solving the whole situation without the need to call in the police.

In my opinion Cox is not correct, however, in his assertion that the primary reason for the failure of the proposals to the black students was their lack of confidence in the administration and their frustration at the University's attitude toward the Harlem community. He gives no evidence to support this view, and I have seen none. Especially in the years when I was dean of the College, I had frequent contact with the black students, the SAS, and the new black fraternity. In none of these contacts did I encounter any comment on the University's attitude toward the Harlem community. I surely was seen by these students as part of the University administration, yet they did not treat me as one in whom they lacked confidence. On the contrary, I have the feeling that they would have looked on me as someone whom they could trust.

My best evidence of this occurred as I was about to leave the University, in February 1969. A group of black students came to my office and asked if I would attend a dinner that they were holding at the Faculty Club. Since I made it a practice to accept student invitations, I readily agreed. It was not until I arrived at the club that I learned that this was a dinner in my honor. About forty were in attendance, including a number of recent graduates, some of whom had come a considerable distance in order to be present. I had a number of compliments paid me as I left Columbia, but none was greater and none moved me more than that one. If they lacked confidence in the University administration, then they did not see me as a part of it.

The University's dealings with this diverse population of "students" were not confined to the weeks beginning with the building occupation on April 23, 1968. Given the deepening tensions created by the increasingly controversial war in Vietnam and given the disposition of many students, especially those subject to the draft, to treat the University as a surrogate for the authorities distant in Washington and to vent their anger and frustration upon it as an available target, and given, finally, the intent of the extremists among them to exploit these attitudes and to attack the University in an effort to convict and to change the society as a whole, University administrators had received plenty of practice over three years in dealing with protests. No two of these were exact duplicates, and responses to them accordingly were not identical. In those years I was frequently asked to comment on student unrest, since I was "an expert." My response always was that though I thought I knew something about where the unrest was coming from, in this matter there were no experts, only veterans. From one campus to another we learned from each other, as apparently the students did also. I remember a telephone call I received from a dean at Cornell after one of our early incidents. He asked what had happened, observing that "Our kids may not be very bright, but they sure are imitative."

REFLECTIONS ON THE COLUMBIA DISORDERS OF 1968

Looking back, however, I can see a certain consistency of policy, at least from my perspective, running through our handling of these cases. This handling was not beyond criticism and certainly was not free of error, but the effort was to remain flexible and to avoid confrontation if possible, and at the same time to defend the functions and the values that seemed essential to the life of the University.

The first of these incidents that I recall came early in 1965, soon after the formation of the Columbia chapter of SDS. A handful of students, members of the chapter, attended without the instructor's permission and with some disruptive effect, one of the classes conducted by the Naval ROTC. I held no strong brief for this program and had grave doubts about its academic quality, despite the fact that the courses were subject to the review of the Committee on Instruction, like all courses in the College, and despite the fact that the credentials of the officers nominated to the program by the Navy were subject to our review and approval. Nevertheless, the long-established tradition that any instructor should have complete control over who might be in his classroom required some action when a complaint of this intrusion reached my office. The students involved were identified and warned, and for several subsequent sessions a member of my staff attended the class to make sure that the incident was not repeated.

Nothing of the sort occurred again (until May 1968, when several incidents of this sort took place in the classes of members of the faculty whom the radical students disliked). At the next meeting of the College Faculty, I reported the action that I had taken in the ROTC case and explained that I had acted as I did because this kind of disruptive behavior was too reminiscent of what had happened in

"THE STUDENTS"—WHO WERE THEY?

German universities in 1933. As I recall, no one chose to discuss the matter in the meeting, but a few days later I received a letter from a member of the history faculty, in which I was taken to task: How could I take the position I had? "These students are not Nazis." Ideology apparently justified otherwise indefensible behavior.

In May 1965, the annual awards ceremony of the Naval ROTC unit, usually held on Low Plaza but that year scheduled for inside Low, was disrupted by a noisy group of demonstrators, mostly the SDS contingent. As I have indicated in the preceding chapter, this incident led to the appointment by the president of the Tripartite Committee on Student Life, whose two years of deliberations, culminating in its report of August 1967, were rather high-handedly treated by the president.

The hope had been, at least from my point of view, that the establishment of this committee would result in the adoption of some acceptable procedures for handling protest and some changes in University organization and practice concerning student participation in making University policies. Its deliberations were prolonged because of a sustained but ultimately unsuccessful effort to win agreement from all five of the student members, only one of whom finally supported it. Though it was a tragic failure, its original purpose was sound.

It was tragic for many reasons, not the least of which was that effectively repudiating the report meant losing the valuable contributions that conscientious students can make to institutional policy. As Douglas Knight has observed, "As long as one does not give them the sole responsibility, one has the right to expect a good deal from mature undergraduates." (Knight, *Street of Dreams*, p. 87) I learned this early in my teaching career, in 1939 at Bennington College, where student involvement in a wide range of substantial matters was taken for granted, and I relearned it at Columbia, if that was necessary, when as dean I arranged for students to sit with the Committee on Instruction, the key faculty committee, as members with all privileges except a formal vote. (As in most such bodies, votes rarely were taken anyhow; the process was one of discussion and consensus.)

During 1966 and 1967 almost all of the incidents, four or five of them, involved attempts to prevent employment recruiting by various corporations and agencies. The Central Intelligence Agency was, of course, a favorite target, as was the Dow Chemical Company, whose destructive products were being used in Vietnam, and the U.S. Marine Corps. No useful purpose would be served by going into details here on all of these. Two general points should be made, however.

First, as these incidents occurred, the University found itself clumsily altering disciplinary procedures, which traditionally had emphasized educational rather than punitive considerations. The alterations increasingly replaced a counseling process with an adversarial process—in my opinion a serious loss—and introduced open hearings in place of closed and confidential ones. They had the advantage of including students as well as faculty and administrators, but by the time of the crisis of 1968 they had not become fully institutionalized. In particular, they had not eliminated the president's final authority in discipline, a provision of the trustees' statutes. In normal times this was a rarely active formality; in the atmosphere of the late 1960s it was highly controversial, especially in the hands of a president who was distant and not regarded with trust by most students. President Kirk contributed to this feeling in at least one instance by not following a committee's recommendations, and it seemed to matter little that one of the exceptions that he made was to allow a student to retain a fellowship despite a committee judgment that it should be cancelled.

Second, recruiting by prospective employers of whom some students disapproved raised some difficult policy problems. Could and should the University deny the opportunity to some and not to other legally constituted organizations? If a student was interested in possible employment by a controversial organization such as the CIA, should he be told that he could not be interviewed on the campus because some elements there disapproved of the organization? I felt strongly that if any recruiting by employers were to be permitted, it should be open to all who had legal standing. I was certain, moreover, that a majority of the faculty and the student body agreed with this position, and subsequent surveys supported that view. But acting on it invited confrontation with the dissenters. Morally as well as politically, what was the proper course?

I favored open recruiting, wisely or not, and the results were mixed. The principle was maintained, but at the price of heightened tension on the campus. The most dramatic example was the attempt to disrupt recruiting by the Marine Corps on April 20 and 21, 1967. It started with a confrontation between the SDS and a group of opposing students in the lobby of John Jay dormitory, where the Marine officers were located. When the confrontation threatened to get ugly, the Marines were persuaded to cancel the day's interviewing and to announce their return on the 21st.

The intervening hours were spent by me and my staff and a number of faculty volunteers devising a system for controlling the flow of students into the dorm lobby where the Marines were to be located, for limiting the number of students in the lobby at any one time, and for keeping opposing groups of students apart in the quadrangle outside. Despite a turnout of about 1000 and an explosive wrangle that lasted for several hours, no violence occurred, and the Marines finished their visit in good order. (I do not know whether any of them were issued battle stars for the engagement, but some of us on the campus thought we deserved one.)

Perhaps more provocative than the insistence on open recruiting was the president's one-sentence policy announcement in September 1967 that aimed at dealing with the troublesome problem, illustrated in the Marine incident, of demonstrations inside campus buildings. This was an issue that had been considered at length in the Student Life Committee, discussed in the preceding chapter. The majority report spelled out a detailed set of regulations to define the limits of such demonstrations. They were aimed at controlling the hazards of such actions and also at achieving an enforceable system. The latter was a daunting challenge, chiefly because of the difficulty in any such demonstration of identifying any but a handful of easily recognized student protesters. Even with cameras, wholesale identification was essentially impossible. The president's statement simply banned all such demonstrations, without explanation, without reference to the Student Life report (which was not released for another seven months) and without consideration of the enforcement problems.

I have already explained why I felt that as a member of the Student Life Committee I could not, in my new position of provost and vice president, "receive" the report. I left it up to the president to act, or, as it turned out, not to act except to issue the unfortunate ban. By hindsight I could and probably should have found a way to intervene and prevent that action. Whether subsequent history would have been changed if I had intervened successfully is debatable. The fundamental atmosphere would not have been altered, and the search for a confrontation by the SDS extremists would not have been ended. It might have made some slight difference nevertheless, and I regret that I did not try it.

The difficulty of enforcing the president's no-indoor-demonstrations rule was matched by a comparable obstacle to all kinds of disciplinary action, namely, that dismissal (of a male student) automatically meant canceling his draft deferment, which required remaining in good standing as a student. A result of these problems was that the enforcement of discipline was uneven, and in consequence, as both Cox and the Luskys have critically noted, the administration of the University appeared weak. (Cox, p. 96; Lusky and Lusky, p. 182ff)

A prime example of disciplinary dilemmas, perhaps the most painful that I recall, grew out of the disruption of the University's memorial service for the Reverend Martin Luther King, Jr., on April 9, the Tuesday following his assassination and two weeks before the building occupation began. It had been my idea to hold the service, and care had been taken in its planning. The president agreed to be present, but to avoid having it appear to be a white observance, we had invited as the principal speaker Dr. M. Moran Weston, a distinguished black clergyman who held both undergraduate and graduate degrees from the University (and who later became a trustee of the University). I made a mistake in not consulting fully with the leadership of the SAS or other black student leaders, but that omission did not directly affect what happened. As the service got under way in a completely filled St. Paul's Chapel, I noticed in the front row on the aisle were seated Mark Rudd and three of his lieutenants. This was a sign of impending trouble, but nothing could be done about it then.

As the service started (not "toward the end of the service," as Cox reports, p. 73) Rudd stepped into the chancel and grabbed the microphone. I was standing nearby and could have tried to take it from him, at the risk of an unseemly tussle and of a real disruption, since, as later appeared, about 40 SDS members were scattered through the audience. I stood aside while Rudd, in the crude and vulgar language that came to him so readily, denounced the president and me and the University and characterized the whole observance as "an obscenity." He and the whole SDS contingent then left the Chapel, and the service continued, but not before the chaplain, John D. Cannon, stated that anyone who wished to speak his mind could speak in the Chapel at any time.

The president was understandably livid, angry at both Rudd and Cannon, and he wanted to proceed against both of them, to discipline Rudd and to have the Episcopal bishop recall Cannon. The latter was a most unpromising line of action, and the former would, in my judgment after I had recovered from my own anger, merely have dignified Rudd with martyrdom. This would have been the case even if it had been shown, by the evidence of leaflets recapitulating Rudd's sentiments distributed outside as he left, that this was no sudden inspiration but a well-planned action, and even though Rudd's disruptive behavior was a violation of New York criminal law.

In the event, no action was taken. Was the University administration weak? That can be argued. It can also be said that given the setting and its circumstances—our commitment to maintaining the open tolerance that must mark a university worthy of the name, the obvious necessity of maintaining some sort of discipline and civility if that tolerance is to survive, the diversity and fluidity of the occupying elements, the ruthless intransigence of the dominant SDS leadership, and our having been cast rather suddenly in the new and uncongenial role of actors through force—we were in a no-win situation.

. . . .

These were "the students." Where are they now? I know the answer for a few, but only a few. One thing is clear about them all, however. None will have forgotten those days of crisis in 1968. Whether they were in the buildings, for whatever reasons, or were outside in the larger group that was protesting the attack on the University; whether they watched from the sidelines or, like many, left the campus until the climax was passed; whether they were connected with schools such as Columbia College, or were in one of the professional schools that stood more or less on the periphery of the disturbance, such as the Graduate School of Business; they inevitably will have memories of Columbia in 1968.

Evidence of the indelibility of these memories appeared in April and May 1988, when the 20th anniversary of the upheaval was observed by a gathering of participants in the building occupation, by a panel discussion at the Center for American Cultural Studies, and at the reunion of the College class of 1968.

The first of these, organized by, among others, the Reverend William Starr, still attached to the Episcopal Campus Ministry, drew Mark Rudd, a teacher in Albuquerque, as its principal speaker. Rudd, as reported in the press, displayed a mix of partial contrition and pathetic arrogance. He was quoted as saying, "Stupidly, we thought revolution was imminent. Our rage blinded us. I now believe that the war in Vietnam drove us crazy." Commenting that he learned more from his "comrades" than from the faculty, he said, "I studied Shakespeare with Lionel Trilling, and I can't remember a thing." And he added, "Many remember it as the best time of their lives. We even tell the story to our kids with pride." (*Columbia College Today*, Vol. 15, No. 2, Fall 1988, p. 30) Two others for whom it seems to have been the best time were Andrea and Richard Eagan, the two part-time students in the School of General Studies whom Mr. Starr married in Fayerweather. Richard Eagan is quoted as saying, "It's something that's made a daily and substantial difference in our lives. That was the most important part of my education." And his wife, still in verbal revolt, with complete assurance said, "The fact is, we were absolutely correct in what we perceived as being wrong. We were in error . . . only in that we weren't successful. (*Washington Post*, April 20, 1988, p. C1)

An interesting feature of the gathering was the considerable number of the company who are now teaching, some of them at Columbia. Many occupations were represented, but teaching was one of the largest. One can't help wondering what goes into the course on the 1960s taught at Fordham by Mark Naison, a member of SDS who

"THE STUDENTS"—WHO WERE THEY?

is now a professor of history. (Some indication of his nonscholarly history is contained in an almost completely fanciful account that he wrote concerning the alleged events that occurred when he took his Ph.D. orals in the spring of 1968. I am indebted to my former colleague, William E. Leuchtenburg, for calling my attention to this bit of spurious nonsense.) Along with some of those who spoke at the gathering, one also cannot help thinking of two of the 1968 actors who could not be present: Ted Gold, who was killed in 1970 while attempting to make bombs; and David Gilbert, who sent greetings to his friends from the prison in Dannemora, New York, where he is serving a sentence of 75 years to life.

At the Center for American Cultural Studies on April 25, the panel included voices from both sides: Lewis Cole, a member of the SDS Steering Committee, who teaches writing for the screen at the Columbia School of the Arts; Eric Witkin, a junior in the College in 1968 and now a lawyer and [for a time] president of the College Alumni Association, a student whom I knew well and one who was stricken by the damage done to his University in the fateful year; William Sales, a student in the School of International Affairs in 1968, who is now a professor at Seton Hall; and three senior members of the faculty—the late Alan Sachs in physics, William Theodore de Bary in Oriental humanities, and James Shenton in history. Judging from the reports, few positions had changed in two decades. Cole and Sales were unreconciled and unrepentant. Witkin condemned the reckless destructiveness of the rebels and was joined by the three senior faculty members. (*Columbia College Today*, Fall 1988, p. 31)

At the reunion of the College class of 1968 a principal speaker was Dr. Paul Vilardi, in the crisis days head of what was called the

Majority Coalition. Now a surgeon, he saw the SDS and their allies as attempting to destroy the institution that would make it possible for him to become a physician, one who could "improve the quality of life for people one at a time." (*Ibid*. p. 32)

Although I knew a large number of Columbia students in 1968 and prided myself on understanding much of the frustration and anger and anxiety that they felt, partly because I shared much of it, the total rejection of civility and reason by some, such as the leaders of the SDS, was almost beyond my comprehension. I still feel that way, but I gained some insight into what made some of them this way when I dealt with some of their parents.

CHAPTER FOUR
ENCOUNTERING PARENTS

I did not deal with a large number of parents during and following the Columbia incidents in 1968. Even had I had contacts in such quantity, I should not expect that the evidence from such exposure would fully account for the shocking breakdown in civility that marked those days. Parental actions and attitudes obviously influence the behavior of offspring, but they are not the only variables. Many parents, I feel certain, were as startled and as disturbed as I was by the actions of "the students"—whether their progeny or not. In those troubled and turbulent times, influences unrelated to parental conduct must in many instances have been the primary determinants of student behavior. Indeed the atmosphere at Columbia that I have discussed in chapter 2 would be sufficient to account for at least a readiness for disruptive behavior; a readiness strongly reinforced by events in the larger community, notably the war in Vietnam.

A number of students undoubtedly were still in revolt against their parents. These were disposed to exploit the circumstances that in their eyes justified rejection of highly visible, and of course immoral, adult authority. Such authority, in the University and in the larger community, provided a ready target for residual hostility to the authority of parents. One did not need to have a scientific sample of

If true, this financial encouragement of disruption may strain one's sense of the acceptable and even one's understanding, but I have no comparable problem with the tender, motherly sentiments of Mrs. Jacob Rudd, who referred indulgently to "my revolutionary," perhaps to distinguish Mark from his older brother, a lawyer in Newark. (*New York Times*, May 19, 1968) It is not much more difficult to sympathize with Mrs. Rudd's coming to the campus in September 1968 to plead, in vain, for the reinstatement of her suspended son, although that reported action attests to a certain indiscriminate permissiveness in the Rudd household.

The most startling and, for me, the most revealing of my contacts with parents was my encounter late in May with a set of people who called themselves the Columbia Concerned Parents Committee. Sometime after the middle of May, I received a request from a representative of the Committee to meet several days later with a delegation from the group. I agreed but asked how many would be in the delegation. When I was told that there would be eight or ten, I readily agreed to have them come to my office in Low Library, since it was a room quite large enough to accommodate a group of that size.

When the appointed afternoon came around, I received a call from the security office (necessary since after April 30 no one was allowed into the building except by way of that office). The officer in charge said that a large group of people indentifying themselves as the Concerned Parents Committee were at the office and claimed that they had an appointment with me. He was calling because they were a much larger group than was indicated on the appointment sheet that my secretary had sent down to Security, apparently 40 or 50. I immediately arranged to make use of the large room used for faculty meetings and sent down word that I would meet the group these as soon as the necessary number of chairs had been set up and arranged. That took 20 minutes or perhaps half an hour.

When I joined the group in the faculty room, I at once apologized for the delay and explained again why it had been necessary. Almost before I had a chance to inquire what they wanted from me, I was treated to considerable verbal abuse for my discourtesy in delaying the meeting and my attempt, as they saw it, to avoid holding the agreed meeting.

I do not have a written record of the meeting, but I have a vivid recollection of its two principal features. The first, their reason for coming to my office, was their demand that disciplinary procedures against their sons be dropped, both those conducted by the newly elected faculty committee and those being prosecuted by the district attorney following the arrests on April 30. They gave me a very hard time on both of these counts and were anything but willing to accept my explanation that these matters were out of my hands. I could not direct or override a faculty committee, and I had no authority to ask that the charges before the courts be dropped.

This was difficult, but my memory of it is much less vivid than my recollection of the second feature of the meeting. This was its almost howling disorder. I have presided over unruly gatherings on more than one occasion, but I have never seen one in which nominally civilized adults were so rude, not just or even primarily to me, but to each other. Almost from the outset they interrupted one another, shouted their disagreements, and generally turned what had begun as a meeting into something more closely resembling a brawl. I suppose that these developments should not have surprised me, since

REFLECTIONS ON THE COLUMBIA DISORDERS OF 1968

I had read press reports of an earlier meeting of the group, or one with the same name, at a Riverside Church auditorium, which had been described as having "erupted in a fist-swinging melee." (*New York Times*, May 3, 1968) Nevertheless, I was unprepared for such a total lack of civility toward each other.

After about an hour this difficult meeting was brought to a painful and inconclusive adjournment. But it was not over, although I did not know that at the time. Early the next morning I had a telephone call from the dean of the Cathedral of St. John the Divine. I assumed it had something to do with the details of the arrangement we had made, and announced a few days before, to hold the Commencement in the Cathedral on June 4, rain or shine, to minimize the possibility of disruption. Perhaps it was something about the technicalities involved in transmitting the ceremonies by wire to five other locations near the campus, since the Cathedral, large as it is, can accommodate the several thousand degree candidates and the faculties, but not family spectators in addition. (That deficiency in the rain facilities was always a source of regret to the University, since a commencement ceremony is a significant family occasion.)

The dean of the Cathedral, however, was not concerned about technical arrangements. He abruptly asked me, "Why did you send that bunch of people down to me last night? I said, "What people? What are you talking about?" He responded that about five o'clock (which would have been a few minutes after the breakup of my meeting) a group of people identifying themselves as the Columbia Concerned Parents Committee had come to his office and had requested that the Cathedral cancel the arrangements for the

Columbia Commencement, saying that they had been sent to him by me.

When I had recovered from my shock, I explained to the dean that I had indeed met the previous afternoon with such a group, that in our discussions nothing whatsoever had been said about the Cathedral or Commencement, and that I most certainly had not sent them to him.

Of the many disheartening experiences connected with Columbia in the spring of 1968, few were more disturbing than this one. The combination of rudeness, prevarication, and unscrupulous psychic vandalism left the last of my illusions in shreds. My shock was so great, and so lasting, that to this day when I encounter a group that calls itself "Concerned" anything, my immediate reaction is strongly negative.

Of course I realized that these people were not representative of all or most parents and that stress and frustration may have led them to take actions that in more tranquil circumstances they would not even have contemplated. But despite my inclination to understand, the fact that any group of Columbia parents could have been so bitterly unscrupulous was decidedly unsettling. I found myself uselessly asking if no member of the committee had voiced objection to this kind of conduct. And I could not help wondering what sorts of examples these parents over the years had set for their sons if as parents they could show such unqualified contempt for the values represented in the society by the University, values that they presumably sought for their sons when they entered the University world.

Those values are fragile, as some members of the faculty also demonstrated during the crisis.

CHAPTER FIVE

THE FACULTY IN CRISIS

The most important, if not the most dramatic, consequence of the 1968 uprising was the splitting and the fragmentation of the faculty. (I refer to the division of the faculty into two camps—three if those few who stood completely aside are included—and I refer to the breaking of friendships, collaborative undertakings, and other relations that reflected the major split.) This consequence was important because the standing and the effectiveness of a university or college depend not only upon the intellectual qualifications of individual members of the faculty but also upon a subtler, far less obvious factor. This is the chemistry of colleagueship, the quality of relations that extend from an individual scholar to his associates. These relations may be few or many, may reach beyond disciplinary lines, or may stay within them. For any individual they do not comprehend the entire faculty, but the set of relations that centers upon that individual cumulates with comparable sets throughout the institution. The cumulated total, its quality and characteristics, essentially defines the institution. The products of the university, its teaching as well as its scholarship and research, thus are the result of individual effort, primarily so, but they also, if only indirectly and, so to speak, by reflection, are collective achievements.

These institution-defining relations mature slowly, and they are inherently fragile. The founders of the many "instant universities" established by the several states after World War II discovered that it is possible to buy academic "stars," to build a handsome new plant, and to recruit good students, but it takes time and experience to develop the collective relations that go to make a good or a great university. The tone and character of these relations, once established, persist in time if they are not disrupted. They become the chief part of the socialization experienced by a new member of the faculty, especially one at the more junior ranks. Subtly they set the terms of his acceptance.

The inherent fragility of these relations derives from two sources. First, a mark of a healthy academic environment is that it thrives on questioning, intellectual non-conformity, and dissent. Challenging received wisdom and questioning conventional opinion are at the heart of creative inquiry. These practices, however, can be disturbing. They call for consideration of divergent views and for self-restraint if dissent is not to degenerate into hostility, as in individual cases it inevitably does. Thus they contribute to fragility as they also stimulate vitality. Second, the relations within the university are essentially if not exclusively intellectual and academic. Deep and inclusive personal relations between individuals may exist, of course, but they are not essential to the enterprise. It is sufficient that one know and live with the intellectual characteristics and preoccupations of a colleague. Beyond these it is not only not necessary to know him; to know or to learn things irrelevant to these intellectual characteristics and preoccupations may be destructive of the conditions necessary to creative dissent.

THE FACULTY IN CRISIS

At Columbia in the spring of 1968, colleagues in the heat of crisis learned things about other colleagues of which, in these terms, it would have been better had they remained in ignorance. What was discovered was moral weakness, betrayal of trust, and a lack of commitment to common values essential to the life of the university as a community.

What was discovered, which should not have been known, could not be ignored. What followed in consequence was not just the destruction of friendships but, more serious in institutional terms, the disruption of the relations of colleagueship. No greater injury than this can be done to a university. It is too high a price to pay for all but the most constructive changes. At Columbia in 1968 it was far too high a price to pay for the essentially trivial results that the disruption produced. Avoidance of such disruption was the fundamental challenge of the 1968 crisis to the University and its administration. That it was not met, at least not fully, was little short of tragic.

"On the Columbia campus during the last week in April [1968] the dominating reality was that the network of relationships and obligations on which some twenty thousand people depended, . . . had been ruptured and was on the verge of irretrievable breakdown." (Lusky and Lusky, p. 254) The rupture referred to in this statement did not include the entire University faculty. It was confined almost entirely to the campus on Morningside Heights; it was even there focused on the arts and sciences, that is, excluding most students and faculty in the professional schools, and within the arts and sciences it was concentrated on the Faculty of Columbia College, especially in the early stages.

Cleavages within the faculty can be described in various ways, but it is accurate to say that a division between those opposing and those supporting the Vietnam War was not primary nor even prominent. This could not be said of the country as a whole and especially of those in the active political stratum. Thus, for example, Walter Lippmann's biographer says, concerning the responses to Lippmann's criticism of the war and of President Johnson's policies in Vietnam, "People who constantly lunched together no longer spoke to one another . . . Lippmann found himself cut off from many he had considered to be his friends. Some openly snubbed him." (Ronald Steel, *Walter Lippmann and the American Century*, p. 579) Differences over the war existed at Columbia, but I daresay that if a vote of the faculty had been taken, a majority—and in the arts and sciences faculty a very large one—would have been opposed to the war.

The SDS tried, and rather skillfully, to make it appear otherwise. Their exploitation of the Institute for Defense Analyses (IDA) and Columbia's participation in it was aimed at convicting the University of complicity in the war. Thanks to a lack of clear University policy on conducting government-sponsored research and, as the Cox Commission notes, a maladroit handling of some faculty questions in 1967 by the then dean of the Graduate Faculties, the late Ralph Halford, they had some success. (Cox, pp. 90–91) Within the faculty these maneuverings did not contribute to faculty trust of the administration, but the war and associated issues did not create a major split in the faculty.

That faculty division was not over the war is illustrated by the signatures on a letter sent without publicity to President Johnson on

May 18, 1966. For several months in 1965–66 ten members of the faculty, of whom I was one, had been meeting to discuss what might sensibly be done to achieve a change in the Vietnam policy. A public protest or an open letter, we recognized, would be futile, serving only to salve our collective consciences. We settled on a long, carefully argued letter, firm but reasoned, critical but not confrontational. (Some weeks later we received a response from the president, also quite long and in comparable tone, but with opposite conclusions.) The signatories included the late Richard Hofstadter, chief drafter of the document, and William E. Leuchtenburg, a staunch and outspoken critic of the building seizures; they also, however, included Alexander Dallin, who ended up opposing the University administration in the crisis, and Daniel Bell, who was one of the key leaders of that opposition.

At the same time it would be inaccurate to say that no members of the faculty reacted ideologically and in full agreement with the extremist students. Some of them did, and not all of these were at a junior level. They and others seem to have regarded the apparent issues as the real ones and to have justified the student actions concerning them.

The fundamental split in the faculty, however, came from a different source. In a typically thoughtful essay published a decade after these disturbances, Edward Shils of the University of Chicago observed that the effective performance of the collective activities that are essential to the performance of the university's intellectual tasks "requires not only administrative organization and authority; it also requires civility—which is concern for the whole—on the part of the academic staff and the students." (Edward Shils, "The Academic discussions they had had many occasions to face the realities, many opportunities to confront the basic dilemma. It was in witnessing these failures or refusals to grasp the fundamental stakes that I learned what I probably should have known without this instructive experience: Character and intellect are not necessarily closely associated. Some of the brightest and some of those with major intellectual reputations turned out to be deficient in the strength to see and to act upon the institutional stakes. As my colleague William E. Leuchtenburg, who later left Columbia for the University of North Carolina at Chapel Hill, said in a letter, "Quite apart from the fundamental issues involved, Columbia was a test in 1968 of how a civilized, mature person behaves under stress, and some did not measure up." (William E. Leuchtenburg to David B. Truman, July 13, 1990) He named no names, but in later pages I shall do so.

An interesting aside: The crucial split between concern for the whole and indifference to it displayed a curious pattern within the faculty, one that I am told appeared also on other campuses. It tended to separate disciplines, in that the "softer" ones and those more abstracted from reality, seemed to be most attracted by the student rebels (or were scattered in all sorts of directions). The more systematic, strongly empirical disciplines tended, on the other hand, to stand with the administration. Few engineers and few physicists, especially few experimentalists, joined the rebels, and the same was true of most of the natural scientists; in the social sciences, anthropology was in full revolt; a large segment of sociology was also, while political science and economics, though divided, had a majority with the administration. History was much like political science. In the foreign languages, the loyalists were in the minority, and in the English department fragmentation was substantial, as was also the case in philosophy.

An early and probably inevitable development after the building occupations began was the gradual evolution of alternative faculty structures, at first totally informal and later partially organized. This was probably inevitable because moves of this sort have appeared on other campuses in crisis, even when instruments for faculty deliberation were in existence and functioning, such as faculty senates. At Columbia, especially with the president's refusal to convene the University Council, the only University-wide instrument in existence, enfeebled though it was, the appearance of alternative structures was all the more likely.

Before this development and contributing significantly to it was the meeting of the Faculty of Columbia College on the afternoon of Wednesday, the first full day of the occupations. The College Faculty, which did not include all faculty in the arts and sciences, was an appropriate body to be assembled, since Hamilton Hall, its principal building, was the first to be occupied and since at that stage most of the occupiers were students in the College. The meeting, held in the large lecture hall of the chemistry building since access to the usual facilities in Low Library was obstructed, was well attended and orderly. The president was in the chair and, after my summary of the events of the past day and a half, a number of resolutions were proposed, the most inclusive by Professor Daniel Bell. Of the five that were adopted, none mentioned amnesty, and one suggested the creation of special disciplinary arrangements to deal with the incidents of the previous two days. In the midst of the discussion, Dean Coleman, who had been held hostage in his office in Hamilton

Early Thursday afternoon I had received word through a faculty emissary that a group of the SDS leaders wanted to speak to me in Low. I went at once to the appointed place. Mark Rudd and two or three of his associates appeared. The meeting quickly became merely a confrontation, as I was told that a guarantee of amnesty was a precondition of any negotiation. It did me no good to attempt to explain why such a guarantee was impossible, and I left the meeting, the last I had with this group, discouraged and depressed.

That same afternoon the president and I held a press conference at which several members of the AHFG were spectators. The president handled most of the questions. He was asked about amnesty and explained why this would make a mockery of university discipline. (It was obvious, of course, that the occupiers could leave the buildings voluntarily at any time essentially without detection and in fact with little or no likelihood of punitive action.) He was also asked about the possibility of police action and responded carefully, indicating that we had moved so far with great restraint because we wished to avoid force if possible and that we would continue to try to do so. He was also asked about the possibility of suspending construction of the controversial gymnasium in Morningside Park and cited contractual obligations as the reason why this could not be done. (I shall have much more to say on this matter at various points in this and later chapters.)

Some of the faculty spectators, apparently feeling that the positions stated at this press conference were too uncompromising, asked me to meet with the group in 301 Philosophy to explain further.

This I was glad to do. I explained in considerable detail the efforts we had been making to negotiate with the various groups in the buildings. On the gymnasium issue I explained as carefully as I could that since we had contracts with builders, with suppliers, and above all with the City of New York under legislation passed by the State, we were not free simply to cancel construction at will, even if we wanted to. I was with the group for about half an hour.

At the end of my discussion, I was asked if there was anything the faculty could do to help, and I responded in the negative, perhaps more bluntly than I intended, but I do not recall feeling impatient or ungrateful. In any event, I have been criticized for this reaction. Since the source in at least one instance is neither hostile nor uninformed, I shall admit that it may be justified and should record a part of it here:

> [I]n ordinary circumstances, David B. Truman would have been fully sensitive to the nuances of faculty temper. . . . Had he not been dog-tired after two virtually sleepless days and nights, he might have realized that the teachers—not fully aware of the administration's efforts and frustrations . . . , and distressed at the rapid and increasing deterioration of the social fabric of the campus—felt a strong obligation to take an active part. Perhaps he counted too heavily on the obviousness of the necessity to close ranks in the face of an assault on the whole concept of rational discourse, and could not believe that the teachers themselves would rebel. In any event, he did not sense the danger. (Lusky and Lusky, pp. 248–249)

I cannot readily comment on these criticisms, not because of any reluctance, but because I cannot recall the range of considerations that guided my actions. I can say, however, that it never occurred to me that "the teachers themselves would rebel." And I can assert that unconsciously but definitely I counted on the understanding and, indeed, the loyalty of men whom I had known well and with whom I had worked for years. In many instances that confidence was well placed; in others it dissolved into illusion. The sequence of events suggests that I should have anticipated a rebellion; it also may suggest that I was perhaps too sensitive at other times to faculty sentiment.

Precisely what happened after I left is not clear, but the weight of testimony is that, as the meeting was about to break up following my departure, Professor Alan Westin of the Department of Public Law and Government (now Political Science) and Professor Walter Metzger of the History Department, each or both, asked everyone to stay and proposed that the faculty should play a role in the crisis separate from the administration. The Cox Commission reports that Westin "remarked that the faculty's admiration for the vice president was blinding it to the need for action on its own part." (Cox, p. 116) In any event it is clear that Metzger asked Westin to take charge, and the group was formed, becoming what one participant characterized as an "association of concerned faculty." (Another "concerned" group!)

This was the formal birth of the Ad Hoc Faculty Group, which immediately set up an executive committee to attempt to mediate between the students and the administration and to prevent what they feared—despite my assurance that no decision had been taken to call in the police—was an impending police action on the campus. The AHFG drew up a resolution containing four points: A request to the trustees to suspend immediately construction work on the Morningside Park gymnasium; a request to the administration to delegate all disciplinary matters concerned with the existing crisis to a tripartite committee, essentially the one set up by the president after the College Faculty meeting; a request that the students evacuate the buildings; and, most important, a statement that "Until this crisis is settled we will stand before the occupied buildings to prevent forcible entry by the police or others." (Quoted in Cox, pp. 116–117)

Although this resolution was widely circulated among the faculty as a petition, I knew nothing of it until at least 24 hours later.

Westin's initiative and the move to set up the AHFG as a separate enterprise were so consequential for all that followed in the next five days that something in more detail needs to be said here about both. Even the Luskys would not, I think, describe it at this point as a rebellion. Nevertheless, this event marked the point at which what many students regarded as the faculty gave legitimacy to the rebels' occupation of the buildings. It was also the point that led men like my colleague Warner Schilling, in his testimony to the Cox Commission, to say, "What turned a crisis . . . into a disaster was, in large part, the behavior of the faculty and in particular the actions of this group."

I had brought Westin to Columbia from Cornell when I was chairman of the Department of Public Law and Government. The department had conducted an extensive search for someone who would carry on a distinguished tradition in public law, and we felt confidence in Westin, partly because he had not only a Ph.D in political science but also a law degree, important because of the department's close and longstanding ties with the School of Law. These were reflected in no fewer than four joint appointments. Although he had performed adequately in the six or eight years that he had been with us, he had not quite lived up to his promise. His research lacked the depth and the quality that we had expected, though it had certain topical visibility and was workmanlike. Nevertheless, both as department chairman and as provost of the University, I encouraged Westin. I also had collaborated with him and three others in producing a textbook, and my wife and I had enjoyed the Westins socially. (A pathetic note: In the midst of the troubles, Mrs. Westin called my wife on the telephone and expressed the hope that the current difficulties would not affect our friendship. We never saw them again.)

Westin was the most conspicuous of a number of Columbia faculty who suddenly discovered students in the crisis after April 23. As the days passed, it became more and more evident that many of these identified with the students and particularly, of course, with those participating in the uprising. These faculty members devoted their energies, at least temporarily, to doing penance for past neglect and to celebrating the idealism of the students in principle while ignoring the contemptuous vulgarity and the destructiveness of their leaders in practice.

The resulting behavior sometimes bordered on the comic. Some days after the police action on April 30 I had a letter from a former student, who was then living in Washington, DC. She had been in the seminar that I had been obliged to give up when I became dean of the College in 1963. In her letter she said that she could not reconcile the criticisms of me that she had read with what had been her experience as a student. She went on to say that she wished that she were dealing at the present in the department with someone like me, because she had sent a draft of her dissertation six weeks before to her sponsoring professor and had not even had an acknowledgment. Because I suspected who was involved, I asked the department secretary who was her sponsor and then passed the student's complaint along to the department chairman. In a few days, I had another letter from the student saying that she did not know what had produced the change, but shortly after she wrote me she had had a note from her sponsor, Professor Westin, commenting on her first chapter and promising to send her his criticism of the rest of the draft at an early date. (I never told her what I had done.)

Whether Westin's initiative in taking over the amorphous group in Philosophy Hall can at that point be called a rebellion is debatable, but it is certain that it contained the seeds of such a development, one that reached full growth after the April 30 bust. To have assumed a posture of neutrality as between the rebellious students and the administration was in fact and in effect to attack the University and to create the split that tragically injured it. It was a large step toward abandoning civility, concern for the whole, a step that may have been gratifying to the ego of the new leadership, especially as down that road Westin heard apparently welcome suggestions that he should become the president of the University. (See transcript of WINS news program, 7:50 a.m., May 16, 1968)

In any event he led the move toward rejection of his former friend. In an interview and a speech on May 1 to the Sidney Hillman Foundation he called for a restructuring of the entire University, including the Board of Trustees. According to the news report, "Mr. Westin criticized the 'power brokers' at the University, and he included David B. Truman . . . for what Mr. Westin said was Dr. Truman's failure to understand the things that students 'in this new generation want.'" And with nauseating bathos, he added that it was "tragic" that "so beloved a personality" as Dr. Truman "did not perceive" that customary methods of dealing with campus groups were no longer effective. (*New York Times*, May 2, 1968) (The failure to understand students probably accounts for the standing ovation given to me by the senior class of the College at the 1967 commencement, and it undoubtedly was aggravated by my practice of keeping several undergraduate advisees both when I was dean of the College and after I became vice president and provost.)

Perhaps it would serve the purpose of attaining a balanced view of what went on among faculty like Westin to note that such conduct was reported on other campuses and by other observers. One of these, a distinguished member of the Harvard faculty, has observed: "I do not remember the 1960s kindly. What went on was brutish and silly and the spectacle of middle-aged men simpering about how much they learned from the young, and flattering the most uncouth of their students as models of intellectual and moral purity, would have been revolting had it not been so ridiculous." (Judith Shklar, "A Life of Learning," Charles Homer Haskens Lecture, American Council of Learned Societies, *Occasional Paper No. 9*, Washington, April 6, 1989) And Irving Howe made a similar comment: "Scenes of turbulence, the mid-60's. Professors who the day before yesterday were the milkiest of liberal or disdained politics entirely now take avidly to revolutionary rhetoric. . . . Enthused academics, recharged intellectuals—I call them, uncharitably, 'guerillas with tenure'—keep telling me, 'The kids are turning the country around.' Turning it where, to what end?" ("The Decade That Failed," *New York Times Magazine*, September 19, 1982, pp. 78 and 81)

The pre-climactic event in the evolution of the Ad Hoc Faculty Group resulted from the seizure of three more campus buildings, making the total now five. Wednesday evening, when, in response to a campus-wide security directive, any attempt was made at 6 p.m. to close Avery Hall, the School of Architecture building, the students declined to leave and, when the normal time of closing, between 10 and 11 arrived, they barricaded themselves in the building and announced their solidarity with the occupants in Hamilton and Low. Early Thursday day morning a group of students broke into Fayerweather Hall, the principal facility for the graduate programs in the social sciences. And around midnight on Thursday a group from Low, reportedly including Tom Hayden and other outside "professionals," seized Mathematics.

The increase in the scale of the uprising was a central concern throughout Thursday, and the president felt compelled to look at the possibility of asking the police to clear the buildings, even at the risk of trouble from Harlem if we proceeded against Hamilton Hall (a problem that I shall discuss in greater detail in later chapters). The seizure of Mathematics was the last straw for the president. Together with a growing ugliness in the mood of the students opposing the occupiers, an ugliness stemming from the apparent inaction of the administration, the seizure decided him for police intervention. I did not dissent from this decision, but I urged him to let me inform the AHFG in Philosophy Hall. Not to do so seemed to me to be something like bad faith, and he assented.

My announcement to the faculty group was probably more abrupt and peremptory than it should have been or I would want. In any event the reaction was for members of the AHFG to array themselves in front of the occupied buildings, to interpose themselves between the occupiers and the police, whom they expected to arrive momentarily. About half an hour later, when a group of police administrators (not uniformed officers) made their way into the security entrance to Low Library, where the president's temporary offices were located, a scuffle occurred in which Richard Greeman, an assistant professor of French, was slightly but rather bloodily injured. The police administrators were there to discuss procedures for clearing the buildings. The questions that they raised, plus the pleading by Westin, Dallin, and others of the AHFG to reconsider the call to the police, led the president to suspend the request.

Accordingly I made an appearance with a bull horn at the Low entrance and announced postponement of the request for police action "while the faculty and the Administration continue their efforts to affect a peaceful solution." I also announced a decision, reached the previous afternoon after some complicated discussions among the trustees, "at the request of the mayor" to suspend construction on the gymnasium. The quoted wording was important, for reasons that need not be explained at the moment. The action, however, was a genuine attempt at calming the atmosphere. It was taken "without prejudice to continuation at a later time," but some of us realized that any such resumption would probably never occur.

My announcement that night has been interpreted by Daniel Bell as telling the AHFG that "finding a way out . . . was now up to them." (Daniel Bell, "Columbia and the New Left," *The Public Interest*, Fall, 1968, p. 78) This is an inaccurate and self-serving judgment. The administration had no intention of abandoning its efforts at a solution or of relaxing its attempts at preventing a split in the faculty. The administration certainly was not about to delegate to an unofficial, self-designated group of faculty, who were threatening to sabotage the University, the responsibility for protecting it. The AHFG was a major part of the problem, not a means to a solution.

Bell's inference underscores the abandonment of civility by him and his associates who embraced the morally ambiguous position of neutrality between the Administration and the occupiers of the buildings. We would have been delighted if through AHFG efforts—or anyone's efforts—the buildings had been evacuated. We did not expect that. What we did expect was that when their efforts were frustrated or rejected, as indeed they were, the AHFG or at least their senior leadership would reject an immoral "neutrality" and restore "civility" to the center of their concerns. Their failure to do so was a tragic and unforgivably cowardly betrayal of the University.

The postponement of the request for police action would have been necessary even without the effort to promote the unity of the faculty in defense of the University. It became clear very early in discussions with police officials that a considerable amount of tactical planning would be necessary if we were to avoid or at least minimize the injuries resulting from police action. The police themselves made it clear, moreover, that an action of the scale that would be necessary could not be mounted before the weekend, when a large anti-war demonstration was scheduled to take place in Central Park. This would call on a large component of police, and until they were freed for other duty, an operation on the Columbia campus could not be scheduled.

Time over the weekend was usefully spent in devising plans for a police action, though no decision was made to put those plans into effect until late Monday. On Saturday we also responded to numerous requests from members of the faculty who were effectively in revolt against the AHFG. These rejected the idea that the AHFG spoke for them and repeatedly requested the opportunity to participate in some enterprise that did represent them.

This recurrent request required a response involving, in the absence of the University Council or a constituted equivalent, some institutional improvisation. We called, by telegram to every affected individual, a meeting of the Columbia Faculties on Morningside Heights for Sunday morning in the large lecture room in the Law School. This was the largest available room on the campus, but it still was not big enough to permit, in addition to the more than 500 faculty who did attend, inclusion of teachers below the rank of assistant professor. Although these were teachers, under the faculty rules they were not voting members of the faculty. Many of them were, however, active participants in the AHFG, and our not including them caused resentment and some protests.

The newly created, extra-legal Columbia Faculties on Morningside Heights, with the president in the chair, received a detailed oral report from me, and the AHFG document, to be discussed in detail shortly, that was not debated or voted upon, and debated and adopted a resolution that had been prepared by a group of senior faculty led by Peter Kenen of economics (now at Princeton) and Sigmund Diamond of sociology. This incorporated the College Faculty resolution by reference, commended the restraint shown by the administration, as well as the steps that had been taken to suspend work on the gymnasium and to revise the disciplinary system, and it re-condemned the building occupation.

No explicit reference was made in this resolution to the possibility of police action. This was my fault. It represents a mistake that I sincerely regret. Before the meeting I was asked by William E.

Leuchtenburg of the History Department to agree to an addition or amendment that would flatly state that if the buildings were not evacuated by a specified time, police action to clear them should be authorized. I do not recall whether I consulted President Kirk about the response to this suggestion. I must have, but I do not recall doing so. In any event, doubting that we had the votes to carry such a resolution, not wanting to contribute to further splitting of the faculty, and not wanting to put us in the position of acting despite a refusal of a large faculty group to support the action, I persuaded Leuchtenburg not to offer his proposal. That was a mistake. Had it been voted, we would have been in a stronger position; had it not, we would have been no worse off than, as things turned out, we were anyhow.

The AHFG document, presented to the meeting by Westin, was the "bitter-pill" resolution, which was prepared by a twelve-man steering committee of the group early Sunday morning. It was in effect an ultimatum addressed to the administration and to the building occupiers. It was the climax of the crisis, not because of its substantive provisions, which were not remarkable, but because of the actions, contemplated and taken, contingent on the responses forthcoming from the administration and the rebel leadership. It set the stage for the ultimate betrayal of the University to which I have already referred.

The document proposed an extensive revision of the disciplinary procedures, essentially granting final authority to a tripartite committee of the sort that had already been established. It also proposed a policy of uniform penalties for all participants in the uprising, thus preventing any special treatment of the leaders of the revolt. Secondly, it proposed an elaborate procedure for handling the gymnasium matter, creating a decision-making panel that would include trustees, faculty, and representatives of the community appointed by the mayor. It would give an effective veto power to the mayor's appointees. Finally, and most important, it called upon the students to vacate the buildings if the president accepted the proposals; it declared the group's intention to obstruct the police if the president did not accept the ultimatum; and it promised not to "further to interpose" the group's members between the students and the administration if the latter accepted the terms and the former did not vacate the buildings. (Text is in Cox, pp. 212–213.)

Because the president could not, without the consent of the trustees, accept these or any other similar terms, the administration spent much of the remainder of Sunday and Monday morning negotiating a response. This was difficult and frustrating, but the details of the effort need not detain us here. What resulted from the president was, on the matter of discipline, a promise to institute a revision of the University statutes dealing with discipline, and, concerning the gymnasium, a commitment to consult with city officials and leaders of the community. In short, it went a considerable distance toward accepting the terms of the ultimatum, though it did not accept all of the details. The president was justifiably serious when he said in his statement, "I am confident that the following decisions carry out the essential spirit of those [the AHFG's] proposals." (*New York Times*, April 30, 1968) He had further reason for confidence in his response because it had been gone over with representatives of the AHFG in advance of its release, and explanations had been given for why the response did not precisely meet the terms of the ultimatum.

From the other side, the steering committee of the building occupiers, after what appears to have been at most perfunctory consideration, rejected the AHFC proposal outright.

This was the turning point. For me, however, the climax was not any of the public announcements, but rather a visit I received late on Monday morning from Alan Westin and Daniel Bell, as leaders of the AHFG. They informed me that they and the group regarded the response from the students as unsatisfactory and the reply from the president as essentially a rejection. I said to them, "Are you telling me that you, as senior members of this faculty and as leaders of your faculty group, will do nothing to support, and may forcefully obstruct, the University administration if it takes the only alternative that now appears to be open to them, namely, to call in the police?" They replied that this was indeed what they were saying. I do not recall what I replied. Whatever I then said, it was the last exchange I ever had with either of them.

They both acknowledged that they were well aware that the hard core of the SDS was not going to vacate the buildings no matter what happened (though most of them had escaped the buildings by the time of the police action). They acknowledged that the administration had no option left but calling in the police and that eventually we would be obliged to take that action, but they nevertheless refused to accept the alternative. Given the loose, genuinely ad hoc character of the AHFG, these two, had they so chosen, readily could have led most of the group to side with the president. They would not face the fact that, while the president had gone a long way toward meeting their suggestions, the SDS leadership was treating them with contempt.

Nor could they face the essential hypocrisy of their "bitter pill" resolution, once they declined to carry out its terms.

This was for me not the most depressing moment of the crisis. That came a day later. But it was the turning point. From then on the search for unified faculty support became futile. Sides had already been chosen. The AHFG reportedly attempted without success to persuade Governor Rockefeller to intervene and to get Mayor Lindsay to act as mediator; and Kenneth Clark, the distinguished psychologist, and Theodore Kheel, the well-known labor arbitrator, worked with the black students in Hamilton, successfully persuading them not to resist police efforts to evacuate them. (They could get nowhere with the radical leadership of the white students.) But the die was cast when the leadership of the AHFG deserted their University.

Attempts to alter this fact by indulgence in fantasy are perhaps understandable, but they do not change the record. In an interview almost 11 years later with Ron Chernow, a responsible journalist, Bell alleged that I was ready to call in the police because I was "under pressure from then-mayor John Lindsay, who feared that the germ would spread to the City University." This is pure invention. Lindsay was in fact reluctant to have the police used for fear that this would result in inflaming Harlem, a point to which I shall return in a later chapter. Bell is also quoted as saying that he and his group opposed "on principle" bringing in the police, a point that may be true, though at the time it was never publicly acknowledged, and he claims to have told me that I "should either shut down the University or go out and argue with the students," a conversation that did not and could not take place, as Bell must have known.

Even more fantastic is his assertion that he counseled me as if I knew nothing of the nature and limits of influence. "I said to Dave," according to this assertion, "the most crucial thing is, authority can't be asserted, it has to be earned." Had I in fact been treated to any such platitude, which I was not, I should probably have responded with some comments on the nature and importance of integrity, of which he was clearly quite ignorant, and on the authority that I had been granted by the students of Columbia when I was dean and by a large fraction of his senior colleagues when I was asked to leave Columbia for Stanford. (Ron Chernow, "Cultural Contradictions of Daniel Bell," *Change*, March, 1979, pp. 12–17)

The inaccuracy, indeed the pure fiction, of Bell's statements to Chernow does not surprise me. Their sleazy indifference to the truth was of a pattern with earlier experiences I had with Bell. In 1963, when I was first dean of Columbia College, I secured a grant from the Carnegie Corporation for the preparation of a report on Columbia's justifiably famous program in general education. By agreement it was to be done by a one-man committee, working in consultation with experienced and involved members of the faculty. Unfortunately, I chose Bell to prepare that report.

The result was a book-length draft document that was so riddled with factual errors and that represented so little research in the record (essentially none), that it utterly failed the purpose of the grant. The faculty Committee on Instruction, who had authorized the study and under whose aegis it would presumably appear, were aghast and were strongly inclined to scrap the whole enterprise. I felt that something could be salvaged from the wreck and persuaded the committee that the effort should be made. A detailed critique resulted in a document, more like a *Fortune* article of the sort Bell had written for years than an academic analysis, published as Daniel Bell, *The Reforming of General Education: The Columbia Experience in its National Setting* (New York, Columbia University Press, 1966).

The full irony of this book debacle and of the betrayal of 1968 was that, as a member of the Columbia faculty I had been responsible, quite directly, for Bell's coming to Columbia from *Fortune*, and thereby starting his academic career. A professorial vacancy existed in the Department of Sociology, and the department was sharply divided over which of two candidates to choose. One camp, favoring Bell, was headed by the late Paul Lazarsfeld, and the other, preferring another man and especially rejecting Bell, was led by the late C. Wright Mills. Both groups asked me to review the dossiers, to talk with all members of the department individually, and to report my advice. I accepted this unorthodox and difficult assignment. The alternative to Bell was a better scholar. Bell was more the showman. Since the position was designed primarily for undergraduate teaching, Bell seemed to me to have the edge, despite the opposition of Mills, who was deeply committed to undergraduate teaching.

So I was, ironically, responsible for giving Bell the opportunity to parlay his escape from *Fortune* into a Harvard professorship and, on the way, to betray the trust that an appointment at Columbia implied. In the discussions during the 1968 crisis, I feared that Bell's ego might prevail over the claims of collegiality. I should have known that would happen.

The emotional low point of the crisis for me occurred on Tuesday afternoon, April 30, at a second meeting of the Columbia Faculties on Morningside Heights, held this time in St. Paul's Chapel because it could be reached from Low Library by way of the tunnels. It had been decided, by whom I do not recall, that it was not safe for the president to appear on the campus; he felt that a report to the faculty was nevertheless in order, and the Chapel was the logical location even though the acoustics were such that those in the rear could scarcely hear the proceedings at the front. I was exhausted, having been up all night, and emotionally and therefore intellectually unprepared for the dispiriting hostility that prevailed in that meeting. It afforded no opportunity for the reporting and explanation that had been the purpose of the meeting. Rather discussion early focused on a resolution that seems to have originated in the Law School Faculty.

Displacing a healing, conciliatory motion prepared by Richard Hofstadter, this resolution was, in fact though not in form, a motion of no-confidence in the president. Presumably because of this implicit meaning, President Kirk yielded the chair. He called upon Dean Warren of the Law School to preside, an unfortunate choice because Warren's verbal facility was limited and his political judgment such that he was not one to resist what amounted to a coup. The key provision of the resolution was to create "an executive committee with power to call the faculty together and to take other needed steps to return the University to its educational task at the earliest possible moment." The committee was to be made up of ten named members of the senior faculty and two junior members to be chosen by the ten seniors. The named members, not surprisingly, included Bell, Westin, Metzger, and Dallin from the AHFG. Westin and Michael Sovern of the Law School became co-chairmen of the group, Sovern soon developing into the dominant partner.

Grayson Kirk's resignation from the presidency of the University did not occur for another three months. For all practical purposes it occurred that afternoon, as the Executive Committee of the Faculty and its chairmen took over a substantial portion of the executive leadership of the University. The whole affair was grossly, brutally unfair. I had been critical of Kirk, but I had been loyal to him and to the University, as had many members of the faculty. He did not deserve the insult he was given that afternoon. The brutal arrogance with which he was treated is illustrated by a comment by Michael Sovern on May 1 in a press conference, held after a meeting with William Petersen, chairman of the Board of Trustees, in which he said, announcing a forthcoming meeting with Kirk, "We're not scared of him." (*New York Times*, May 1, 1968) The University, moreover, did not deserve the added divisiveness that was created by that session in the Chapel. Perhaps I should have asked for the floor and attempted to make these points before a vote was taken. (I might at least have been able to let those in the rear of the Chapel hear what was taking place.) But frankly I did not have the strength of spirit to try.

I too felt that I was repudiated, but my own fortunes were not important. I had long since decided that I would have to resign after a police action, though I was determined that the resignation would occur only when I chose to submit it. And in the interim I committed myself to doing everything I could to restore calm and purpose to Columbia's existence.

Rather quickly the executive committee established themselves with the trustees. Among other things they secured Ford Foundation funding for the creation and functioning of the Cox Commission, though the president formally accepted the grant. According to one presumably reliable account, they also, during the summer of 1968, while advising the trustees after Kirk's resignation, "devised criteria for the selection of an acting president that deliberately excluded Truman." (Elinor Langer, "Columbia University: Still at the Crossroads," *Science*, November 22, 1968, pp. 878–883) After Andrew Cordier became acting president, Sovern as chairman of the committee—Westin having been defeated in a re-election contest in mid-May—attended the president's daily meetings of deans and top administrative staff and participated as a full member.

The deep divisions within the faculty were evident and visible for a considerable time. As Elinor Langer observed in *Science*, late in November 1968, "beneath the surface all is by no means well. . . . The bonds that make a university a community—shared values, a conviction of high purpose—have worn very thin." The blurred vision that had marked the flounderings of the AHFG, which split openly on May 1, persisted in the mock commencement held on Low Plaza while the official one was taking place in the Cathedral. A number of dissident faculty members, not all of them of junior rank, participated in the mock proceedings. These were addressed by, among others, Harold Taylor, former president of Sarah Lawrence College, Dwight Macdonald, Erich Fromm, and Alexander Ehrlich, a Columbia economist. In mid-May members of the Law Faculty issued a statement condemning the student uprising and defending the decision of the University administration to call the police, but a minority of the members declined to sign it, among them Michael Sovern. Professor William E. Leuchtenburg, in a letter of July 1990, to which I have referred early in this chapter, said that the Columbia crisis "remains a burning ember for me. . . . [T]here are some people I never spoke to again after that spring and there are certain names that only have to be mentioned to me and my gorge rises." Nearly a year after the crisis was over Professor Marvin Harris of the anthropology department denounced dean of the College Carl Hovde for a statement declining to repudiate an issue of the alumni magazine, *Columbia College Today*, that the editor devoted entirely to an account of the whole crisis from his perspective. (I had by then announced my resignation, but I decided I would not ignore this attack and in a letter to the *Columbia Spectator* I denounced it as "an act of blind bigotry" and "an example of the authoritarian madness" that Harris had indulged in for ten months. The metropolitan press picked up the story, and I received quite a run of approving letters.) (*New York Times*, February 20, 1969)

Post-mortems began to appear soon after the events of April and May, rationalizing or at least attempting to analyze and report. Those written by participants rarely reported any second thoughts, and none that I saw indicated any changes of heart. That apparently required the perspective possible after a considerable period of time, and even after 20 years comprehension did not necessarily include a full awareness of what was implied in the positions taken during the crisis. Thus Walter P. Metzger, professor of history and a founding father of the AHFG, has been quoted as saying, "I got caught up in those events without knowing what I was doing. I was sleepwalking. I sentimentalized the students beyond belief." This reads like recognition of the incompatibilities inherent in the AHFG position as well as awareness of having been manipulated by the SDS Steering Committee. If the regret is real, however, the awareness is not discerning, for he further pleads, "But there was one thing I didn't want to happen. I didn't want police to come on campus and use their billy clubs." (Morris Dickstein, "Columbia Recovered," *New York Times Magazine*, May 15, 1988, p. 34) Only those who at the time saw what was at stake could afterward know what had been abandoned. Thus professor of government Joseph Rothschild, who had argued in the AHFG that to attempt to be neutral was to betray the University, could say with conviction, "Our faculty group was rising above principle to expediency. We acted like value-free mediators in a labor dispute. (*Columbia College Today*, Spring 1968, p. 36)

CHAPTER SIX

THE PRESIDENCY IN CRISIS

Any somewhat introspective chief executive must from time to time hope that the circumstances in which he finds himself will not expose his limitations and exploit his weaknesses. Whether his sphere is public or private, political in the strict sense or merely subject to general scrutiny and consequently political in a broader, functional sense, he is likely to feel this concern or anxiety, especially in rapidly changing circumstances.

The campus upheavals of the 1960s, particularly the late 1960s, were of this order. They suddenly confronted most college and university presidents with a sharply altered set of conditions and a collection of problems not readily susceptible to solution through the methods of consultation, discussion, and reason that are the established norm in such institutions. Presidents who with these methods had operated acceptably or even with high success suddenly found that their customary modes of operation did not work, and in some instances were woefully inadequate. Many of these men were hurt, their reputations severely damaged. Some were confronted with circumstances so intractable to any rational handling that they were bound to lose no matter what methods they attempted to use. Others simply found that their managing styles and the accumulation of negative perceptions resulting from years of exposure to those styles rendered them completely unequal to the crises that they suddenly faced. That was the experience of Grayson Kirk at Columbia.

I do not know if Kirk ever felt these introspective anxieties. If he did, he would never have told me or, probably, anyone else. But the crisis from April 23 onwards fed on the accumulated problems of his presidency and revealed the weaknesses and some of the strengths, especially the former, of his presidential operating style.

I need not repeat the details of the sketch of Kirk that I presented in chapter 2. In summary, his style was to preside but not lead, to reign but not rule, and increasingly over the years he became, or, what is the same thing, seemed to become remote and two-dimensional, one who enjoyed the prestige of his position but did not work very diligently at it. It is not inaccurate to say that in personality and manner he was not suited to the assignment of dealing with a crisis of this sort. Given the background provided by practices at Columbia in the years leading up to the crisis, which I have already discussed, one may question whether any style of operation could have met the 1968 crisis successfully. What is certain is that the Kirk style was not it.

Essentially what must be said of Kirk's performance in the days following April 23 is that he did not take charge. Yet the challenge to the University that developed in those days required leadership that only a president could give. He did make decisions when they were asked of him, but he did not take over. If it be said that had he given a stronger and more visible lead in the crisis, he would have become the prime focus of the protest, the response would be that because of the background events, he was a major focus of the protest anyhow. Thus, with respect to the controversy over the Institute for Defense

Analyses, in which Kirk as well as Columbia were active, the Cox Commission accurately observed (p. 92) that "the University Administration . . . treated the problem of secret war research more casually than its intrinsic difficulty and emotional impact deserved." And on the question of student discipline and student participation in that process, Kirk's much criticized failure to respond for nearly ten months to the report of the Committee on Student Life was more significant to the crisis than his belated acceptance of a tripartite disciplinary structure after the buildings had been seized. Even the *New York Times*, which had been editorially supportive of the University during the troubles, commented, "It is no credit to Columbia's own sensitivity to the ferment on every campus that such machinery is only now being created—under crisis conditions." (*New York Times*, April 29, 1968)

It is difficult, indeed next to impossible, to reproduce in all their complexities and nuances the decisions that were made in the course of the crisis. But a chronological recital of some of what seem to me to be the most important of them can suggest both their character and Kirk's role in them.

When, on the first afternoon, Hamilton Hall was seized and Dean Coleman taken captive in his office, I reached Kirk by telephone in a meeting somewhere downtown and explained the situation. His immediate reaction was that we should call the police in and evict the occupiers. When I argued that this would be a mistake, his response was that I was present on the spot and I should do as I thought best.

The decision that I made became controversial, although the Cox Commission concluded (p. 157) that it was the right one. I do not know how Kirk felt about it later, but the pertinent point is that, although he was criticized for not going in at once, to my knowledge he never publicly stated disagreement with what I had done or reported that I had dissuaded him from his view that we should call the police immediately.

Much the same could be said of his decision on the night of Thursday–Friday, April 25–26, to abort the police action precipitated by the seizure of the Mathematics Building, the fifth to go, as I have explained in chapter 5. He readily acceded to my request that I be allowed to inform the AHFG meeting in Philosophy Hall, and when that message provoked a plea from members of that group to cancel the action, he agreed that I could announce a suspension of the request. That really meant a deferment of four days, as it turned out, and criticism from some quarters was substantial. Thus, reviewing the whole crisis some weeks later, a reporter for the *New York Times* (June 10, 1968) referred to "the administration's failure to move for the entire week following the start of the uprising." The criticism was not wholly unjustified, as I admitted in an interview quoted in the same article: "We allowed the activity of the demonstrators to become customary and accepted." I think the calculated risk we took was warranted. My impression, moreover, was that Kirk felt the same way, for he never indicated later to me or, as far as I know, to anyone else, that he thought I had misled him.

Kirk was not inflexible, even though he was not usually disposed to take the lead. For example, on Thursday morning, April 25, I had a telephone call from Kenneth Clark. We were friends, in part because his son had been a student in the College when I was Dean. Ken called to ask if there was anything he could do. I welcomed his interest, both because of his skill and wisdom and because, as a highly respected black, he indeed might get through to the students occupying Hamilton, since they might be prepared to trust him.

I gave Ken the Hamilton phone number and urged him not to mention me, as that might handicap his efforts. I heard nothing from him until sometime on Sunday, when he told me that he had gone into Hamilton on Saturday night, had talked to the students, and had gotten nowhere. He wanted to think further about the problem, and on Monday morning he called me and said that he had been talking with various people, including Theodore Kheel. They had come up with the idea that Ken and he would go in as officers of MARK, Ken's action agency in Harlem. I checked with Kirk, who said something to the effect of "We can live with this; tell him to go ahead." (When I was asked by the press about Kheel's presence on the campus, I denied knowing anything about it.)

Clark and Kheel did get into Hamilton on Monday and talked with the students. They were told, in response to their direct question, that Clark and Kheel were not wasting their time, at which point they said that they would put the same proposition to Kirk and me. It was essentially a proposal about handling the gymnasium issue, about discipline and assurance against certain kinds of penalties, but not amnesty. The students, insisting on their private deliberative procedures, requested permission to have until 8 p.m. Monday night to give their decision. We of course agreed. At 8:15 Clark called and said that the students had called and asked for an extension until nine. I then told Ken that the clock was ticking, that the necessary advance warning had been given to the police, but I said yes to nine and more time if they needed it, because the president had agreed that if we could get an agreement with the students in Hamilton, we might be able to solve the whole thing without the police. Nine came and went, as did ten. About 11 Ken called and said he was terribly sorry, but the Hamilton students had said no. (Clark and Kheel also asked that the police action be deferred indefinitely, so that they could attempt further mediation, but they had no concrete proposals, and in consequence the president was unwilling to grant their request.)

Kirk did not resist the request of an informal AHFG committee that on Thursday morning, April 25, asked him to set up a tripartite committee on discipline, as proposed by vote of the College Faculty on the previous afternoon. He constituted the three faculty members who brought this request—Professors Galanter, Hovde, and Trilling—an ad hoc committee to propose the composition and the powers of the administration-faculty-student committee. The request came to him. However, he did not initiate action immediately after the College Faculty had voted.

Quite early in the crisis, it became obvious to me that something needed to be done to defuse the gymnasium issue, even though construction at the Morningside Park location had already begun. Kirk agreed and undertook to get the concurrence of the trustees, which was forthcoming, since all that was asked for was suspension and since it had been arranged that we could assert that the action was being taken "at the request of the mayor." This was essential, or thought to be, since it protected the University from action under the contract with the city to build a joint-use structure.

Further dealings with the trustees were not so simple, notably in our efforts to meet the "demands" of the AHFG's "bitter-pill" resolution, which I have explained, along with the president's response, in chapter 5. I joined the president at several of the many trustee meetings, held downtown at the University Club because their assembling on the campus would have been at best provocative. But the crucial meeting on these "demands" I did not attend. During those meetings when I was present, it was rather embarrassing because members of the board would listen to the president, and then frequently one or more of them would say, "What does Dave think?" My message was not materially different, of course, but I did not like functioning as a kind of court of appeal from the president's advice.

During the crucial meeting that I did not attend, Kirk called me on the phone and said that he had not been able to persuade the board to accept what he and I had agreed were minimum concessions concerning revision of the University statutes on discipline and on the process for deciding whether to abandon the gymnasium. Would I talk, by phone, to some of the trustees who wished to hear my arguments? I would and did. I don't recall exactly what I said, but I tried to be as eloquent as possible and in particular to emphasize that, unless major concessions were made in these areas, there was no hope of winning over the leaders of the AHFG and, in consequence, of avoiding the police action. I also do not remember exactly which trustees I talked to, but they included the chairman, William E. Petersen, and especially my good friend Harold F. McGuire, a distinguished lawyer who chaired the gymnasium committee. With the latter in particular I recall getting so worked up that I very nearly broke into tears. In any event, I convinced them that without the approval we had no hope of carrying the AHFG with us and of retaining their support if the police action became necessary.

Planning for the police action which eventuated in the first "bust" of Monday–Tuesday night, April 29–30, was begun as early as

Sunday. It was on a contingent basis, since we could have called off the action up to about 30 minutes before it took place, if we so decided. But it had become clear to us and to the police command that careful planning would be necessary to minimize the risk of injury to anyone. In particular, we explored the ways of entering several of the buildings through the maze of heating tunnels that underlay the campus. This could be and was done in two of the buildings, Hamilton and Low, but it was not feasible in the others, which meant that instead of having the (unintended) protection from the outside against those who were picketing these buildings, the police had to break through those ranks. That necessity, of course, maximized the radicalizing effects of the police action. Five "clean" actions from inside would have reduced the numbers involved, made the appearance of police violence much less prominent, and made the reaction to the police less extreme.

The essentials of all of these plans and the consequent actions were known to and approved by the president. But in no case was the initiative his. At no point did he question the contingencies or amplify them, challenge the plans, or suggest actions in dealing with their consequences.

Lest the point about the president's failure to take charge be made too stark and hence unfair, however, I should emphasize that the president did not relish the prospect or the fact of police action, though some of his critics and some of the press treatments suggested the contrary.

Few commentators, before or after the crisis, discussed the problem raised by the presence of police on a university campus as clearly as Max Lerner:

> Except in the most extreme situations, they have no business there. It would be hard to find a college administrator, including Kirk and Truman, who would disagree with that. But can anyone deny that that had become an extreme situation? To make an absolute of the taboo on police would be to throw away the final safeguard that any community—including a university—must have against the kind of direct action that destroys a community. But also the invoking of police force erodes the trust without which no university community is possible. There is the nub of the Columbia agony. Without the police the university would have had to be written off. (*New York Post*, May 3, 1968)

I am confident that Kirk understood this, at least in general terms, even if the likes of Westin, Bell, and the other leaders of the AHFG did not. Intellectually and emotionally I understood it, although, as I observed in chapter 5, my caution, influenced at least unconsciously by respect for the taboo, led me to pass up what was my best and last chance to induce a substantial number of faculty to join in facing the alternative, when I persuaded Professor Leuchtenburg before the Sunday morning meeting of the Morningside faculties not to propose a resolution authorizing police action.

A final, important decision in the 1968 spring series was made at a critical point by the president and with most unfortunate consequences. This was in connection with the so-called second "bust" on May 21–22. It was precipitated by the refusal of five students—all SDS leaders—to appear in response to a summoning letter from the dean of the College, issued in pursuance of the procedures adopted by the new Joint Committee on Discipline, which included automatic suspension for refusal to respond to a dean's summons. The students involved were Mark Rudd, Nick

Freudenberg, Morris Grossner, Ed Hyman, and Ted Gold. A protest rally at the Sundial was followed by a move into Hamilton Hall by 200 or so, including some of the students' parents and lawyers. While the associate dean was talking with the latter, who did not remain in the building, a conference in the president's office led to Dean Coleman's directing the occupants to vacate, on pain of arrest and suspension. A number did leave in the course of the evening before the police arrived, but a number remained, and it was during this period that a fire broke out in the office of history professor Orest Ranum, destroying many of his notes and records. The office was ransacked before the fire was set. The police once more came through the tunnels, the demonstrators—this time including Rudd—were arrested without incident.

The emptying of Hamilton was followed by a good deal of rampaging around the campus, presumably by frustrated demonstrators. The brick walks became a source of ammunition, and before long a number of bricks came through the huge glass windows in the Low Library offices, where the president and others were conferring. (The Paris riots had intervened since the first "bust," marked by the customary use of paving stones for projectiles. Walking across our campus on one of these days, I had said to a colleague, "I wonder when our demonstrating students will discover the parallel usefulness of our brick walks?")

With glass flying in Low and with reports coming in of fires and the breaking of windows elsewhere on the campus, the president made a crucial decision. Against the advice of the associate dean of the College, Alexander Platt, who had been out on the campus and was convinced that the violence was subsiding, he directed a request to Chief Inspector Sanford Garelick, who was in the building to clear the campus. The results were the ugliest of any incidents in the whole series. Undeniably there were incidents of police brutality, and, although no demonstrators were injured seriously, the campus was further radicalized.

The pattern that runs through these decisions by the president was a failure to lead, punctuated by occasional responses to challenge that were almost impulsive reactions, and marked by a stubbornness and frequently an insistence on technicalities. When he was obliged or persuaded to modify some of the latter, he gained little in credibility and nothing in leadership stature.

In my opinion the most disastrous of his stubborn refusals to act was his absolute and immovable rejection of the proposal to convene the University Council and to consult with its members, a majority of them elected by the faculties, on the confrontation. I have discussed this hostility to the council and the reasons for it in chapter 2. I need not repeat them here.

I should point out, however, that Kirk was not consistent in his attitudes toward the University Council, judging from his actions in an earlier but not wholly unrelated situation. In January of 1966 the College Faculty, of which I was then dean, voted to request the University administration to discontinue the practice of reporting the class standings of students to local Selective Service Boards. The action was a response to strong student demand and represented also a conviction by a large majority of the faculty that their grading of students should not be an instrument for draft boards to make their decisions. This vote was reported immediately to the president, without result as far as the dean's office was concerned. Meanwhile student agitation persisted. On March 9, 1967, the president announced that he was calling a special meeting of the University Council to consider the question, and two weeks later the council unanimously voted to withhold class rankings from draft boards. (A subsequent action by the trustees will be discussed in chapter 7.)

Why the president decided to use the University Council in this case, I do not know. I was not involved in the decisions in Low Library in that period. My guess, however, is that the then vice president, Lawrence Chamberlain, persuaded him to employ the council. I doubt very much that Kirk spontaneously and without such persuasion turned to the council, but I do not know what led him to take this unusual course. Nevertheless, however his resistance was overcome, his turning to the council in this controversial and highly visible situation constituted a strong precedent for its use in the 1968 crisis, had he been willing to do so. He was not.

He seemed to be wholly unaware that without some such institutionalized body, the presidency had no insulation from the kinds of attacks that grew out of the 1968 crisis. Nor did he anticipate that the authority of the office subsequently would have no protection, especially given his management style, against the preemptive actions of the Executive Committee of the Faculty, set up in the second meeting of the faculties on Morningside, which I have discussed in chapter 5. As this development amply illustrates, the improvising of the Columbia Faculties on Morningside Heights was no substitute for the institutional vehicle that the University Council might have been.

Kirk was persuaded, however, as the likelihood of a police action began to seem greater, to add three appointed members of the faculty to the group meeting with the president. These were Polykarp Kusch, professor of physics and a Nobel laureate, William Carey, professor of law, who had been chairman of the Securities and Exchange Commission under President Kennedy, and Alexander Dallin, Adlai E. Stevenson Professor of International Relations. These three met frequently with the president and his immediate staff. (Dallin dropped out before the final decision was made to summon the police. For personal reasons that I suspect are traceable to memories of family experiences in Czarist Russia, he could not countenance, much less be a party to, the use of police on the campus. On the night of the "bust," knowing what was coming but honor-bound not to reveal what he knew, he disappeared, to the concern of his colleagues and the considerable distress of his wife. He was finally located in his office in the School of International Affairs. One of the costly casualties of the 1968 crisis, he resigned a couple of years later to accept an appointment at Stanford.)

Having these respected faculty members sit with the president when the crucial decision was made was not a bad idea, but the device did not and could not supply the legitimacy to his decision that might have come from the University Council, especially as no attempt was made to exploit the public relations value of the arrangement. Significantly, the Cox Commission report does not mention their participation.

The area of student discipline and proposed revisions in pertinent University statutes and procedures illustrates Kirk's tendency to rely initially on technicalities to justify a resistance to change and then under pressure to back away with a loss of stature and no gain in influence. In early May a faculty-student-administration committee that came to be known as the Joint Committee on Disciplinary

Affairs, appointed by the president after the crisis, made its report after two weeks of intense deliberation. It was a constructive report, firm but fair and aimed at creating an orderly decentralized system. (It was this system's operation that resulted in the second seizure of Hamilton Hall on May 21.) The president's immediate public reaction was to reject two pivotal proposals: first, that the University drop trespass charges against those arrested on the night of April 29-30 and, second, that the president agree not to increase any penalty assigned by the Joint Committee acting in its appellate capacity.

To the first of these, the initial response was that the University did not have the legal power to drop criminal trespass charges once they had been lodged. This was technically correct and, with the district attorney of New York County, Frank Hogan, a member of the Board of Trustees, it was an understandable but avoidable response. To the second proposal, the first response was simply that it was unacceptable. The Cox Commission (p. 127) reports that the president was under explicit instructions from the trustees not to relinquish his ultimate disciplinary power granted by the University statutes, a point that I shall deal with in chapter 7, but, even granting that point, I doubt that he was obliged to respond as peremptorily as he did in his first reaction to the Joint Committee's proposal.

The Committee's reaction, through its chairman, Quentin Anderson, professor of English, was one of disappointment and some bitterness, as some members of the Committee threatened to resign. The next day Kirk, speaking through the press representative of the Executive Committee of the Faculty—a point of considerable significance in itself—yielded on the matter of his disciplinary authority by saying that if he disagreed with the committee he would submit the matter to arbitration by a distinguished alumnus acceptable to both parties. And on the trespass question George Fraenkel, the dean of the Graduate Faculties, who had become the president's unofficial press spokesman, let it be known that the University was seeking ways to avoid prosecution of students under the criminal trespass charge.

However one wants to interpret this incident, it is impossible not to conclude that the president emerged from it with his authority and position weakened.

The record of the president's relations with the Executive Committee of the Faculty compels a similar inference. He tolerated and submitted to a set of preemptive actions by the committee, in effect letting them take over the presidency in all but name. The day after it was formed (an event that I have already dealt with in chapter 5) the committee issued a statement calling for dropping all criminal charges against students who had been arrested the previous morning. On the same day it met with the president. I was present and recall that it was largely pro forma and involved no substantive plans or proposals. Nevertheless, the *New York Times* the next day (May 2, 1968) quoted "a source close to the committee" as saying that Kirk recognized the committee as the only body that could take action to restore the University to normal operation and to propose long-range changes. "He has legitimized the committee, not only by his presence at the time of its creation, but through meeting with the committee this afternoon, the source said."

The president had no part in securing foundation financing for the Cox Commission, other than possibly giving his oral consent to the foundation's action after the committee had already secured a commitment of funds. I do not know exactly what occurred, as I was not privy to the president's actions at that time. When the commission was announced with some fanfare on May 5, Michael Sovern, professor of law and co-chairman of the committee, stated to the *New York Times* that "he had informed Dr. Kirk of the commission's creation by telephone and that 'he was grateful for my informing him.'" (*New York Times*, May 6, 1968) If that statement were interpreted as an insult to the president, the interpreter could not be accused of over-sensitivity.

Kirk never testified before the Cox Commission. Whether his not doing so was a mistake on his part can be debated. He was such a controversial figure by that time that many of his staff were of the opinion that his appearance before an open hearing would have provoked a riot. In particular, the late Ralph Halford, former dean of the Graduate Faculties and in 1968 assistant to the president for special projects, who was probably the most cautious administrator I have ever known, counseled strongly against Kirk's testifying. His caution fit the president's inclinations.

I was in on these discussions and I did not argue with the fears expressed. I also agreed to be the administration's principal witness at the hearings. Had I been in Kirk's place, however, I would have insisted on finding a way to appear before the commission. To have done so might not have reestablished his leadership and might have been acutely embarrassing, but at least it would not have reinforced the damaging appearance of aloofness or indifference. It also might have helped to offset the impression that the presidency had been replaced by the Executive Committee of the Faculty. In any event he did not take the risk.

THE PRESIDENCY IN CRISIS

It would be inaccurate and unfair to imply that the president made no effort to reassert his leadership after the police action or to propose means of healing the rifts that had split the University community. Guided in part by recently retained professional assistance (a change that I shall discuss further in chapters 7 and 11), he held a number of press conferences aimed at both of these objectives. Early in June he issued "A Message to Alumni, Parents, and Other Friends of Columbia," which gave an account of the crisis and raised and then responded to a series of questions about what had happened, what he anticipated for the future, and what he saw as the larger implications of the uprisings.

On at least one issue connected with the affair he took a public position that was courageous and anything but vindictive. To proposals in Congress and in the New York legislature to withhold government financial aid to students who participated in campus uprisings he expressed firm and unqualified objection. "Any attempt," he declared, "by governmental authorities to deprive these offending students of financial aid which they are now receiving under federal or state programs would be difficult to administer equitably and would pave the way for the adoption of tests of political orthodoxy that would endanger the freedom of opinion and expression which all universities cherish." (*New York Times*, May 14, 1968)

These efforts, however, tended to be defensive rather than constructive, and they did not reach out into the faculty, where, at least in my opinion, the damage had been greatest and where the need for healing was most critical. Above all, these actions did not change his essential operating style, because they could not.

REFLECTIONS ON THE COLUMBIA DISORDERS OF 1968

That style is illustrated by an event that occurred on the evening of Friday, May 17, one that is worth recalling in some detail for a variety of reasons. The Kirks had driven to their University-owned weekend establishment in Millbrook, New York. Late in the day, my wife and I were driving up the Taconic Parkway toward our cottage in Hillsdale, New York, which we had not been able to visit for more than a month. Both couples were in need of a break for rest. As we were driving through Northern Westchester, about 6 p.m., my wife decided to turn on the car radio, thinking that hearing the news would be a pleasant distraction. What came over the radio was not pleasant and not a distraction from my worries. It was an announcement that a group of Columbia students, led by Mark Rudd, and some neighborhood people had seized an apartment building at 618 West 114th Street, just west of Broadway. Owned by the University, the building was in the process of being converted to University uses, and its remaining tenants were being gradually relocated.

I immediately pulled off the parkway into a service station, from which I telephoned the campus. I was informed that Kirk had been notified and that he had said he would come in if necessary. Those on the campus reported that police assistance for the evacuation had been called for, as we had planned in such a contingency. Perhaps I should have given the same response as Kirk had, but it seemed to me improper for the top officers of the University to be off on a weekend when what might be a serious incident was taking place on the campus. So I said I would return as fast as I could, and we headed back down the Taconic.

When I reached the campus, I found that the police had set up a command post in a garage on Broadway at 114th Street. I also learned that my son, who was then teaching at Yale, had also heard the news reports and wanted to come down to help. Although my wife assured him that there was nothing he could do, he and his wife, plus their little dog, got into their car and drove down from New Haven. I was at the police command post when he walked up from our apartment.

The police moved slowly and methodically in preparation for clearing the building. They preferred, as usual, to wait until the early morning hours, when as few people as possible would be on the streets. As the police vans were assembled, the imminence of a removal action became obvious; abusive shouts came from the roof of the adjacent student center, and there was a good deal of pedestrian traffic on the walk past the garage. For a while I stood in the doorway to watch the proceedings, but when I was recognized I was treated to such a storm of verbal abuse, spitting, and physical threats that it became prudent to withdraw inside. At one point my son said, "Dad, I've never heard people talk to anyone the way they did to you."

The police began their action about 4 a.m. initially ordering demonstrators inside and outside of the building to move west toward Riverside Drive or face arrest. Many did move. Among the remainder, there was no resistance, inside or outside the building; 117 were arrested, about half of them Columbia students, including Mark Rudd. The whole operation was over by about 5 a.m. I waited around for a time until it was certain that things were quiet, after which my son and I walked down the hill to our apartment building for some breakfast and a few hours of sleep. His presence and his bringing his family from New Haven to stand by us made a distasteful and unwelcome experience somehow not only tolerable but deeply moving to me. I doubt that they can ever know what their insistence on being present meant to me, in particular, and to my wife. Later in the morning, President Kirk issued a statement to the press thanking the police.

Peculiarities of presidential styles, accentuated by crisis, have consequences for the institution, for those immediately associated with the president, and for the chief executive himself.

For the University, Grayson Kirk's preference for presiding without leading, for reactive management that was sometimes unconstructively impulsive, resulted in institutional drift and, in the face of a challenge to the institution, a weakened central authority.

The failure of a substantial number of faculty, especially senior professors in positions of influence and prestige, to see the threat to the University and to recognize no identity of interest between themselves as individuals and the collective enterprise is not forgivable. That failure merits only a mixture of pity and contempt. But it must at the same time be recognized as in part a product of the drift and decline that are fostered by unperceptive and ineffectual leadership. Even men lacking in character are unlikely to sabotage and desert an enterprise that is generally held in high esteem and is perceived to be collectively in creative motion.

Drift and decline result under crisis conditions in divisions, hostilities, and increased demoralization that persist for years. These things did occur at Columbia in and after 1968; I could see them. How far they have persisted in time I cannot know for sure, as I have not been a participant since 1969, but what I do see and hear leads me to the conclusion that recovery after more than two decades is far from complete.

THE PRESIDENCY IN CRISIS

On the consequences for the president's immediate associates, I can best testify for myself. I had been vice president and provost of the University for barely ten months when the crisis occurred, but I was the second-ranking officer of the University and thus exposed to its risks and to its results.

Grayson Kirk apparently understood clearly my exposure. Again and again, especially during the week of April 23 through 30, he said, to me and to others who reported his statements to me, "I do not want anything in this to hurt Dave Truman's career." I have no reason to doubt the sincerity of his intentions, and it may well be that in the circumstances nothing he could have done would have provided the protection implied by his expressed intent. But if he wished to minimize the damage to which he referred, he should have taken the visible lead and conspicuously kept me in the shadows. I realize how difficult that would have been, since it would have required him to take charge in a strong and consistent fashion that would have been quite out of character, and it would have been essentially impossible to eliminate my accessibility to faculty and others, since my whole record, as colleague, as department chairman, as dean, and briefly as provost, had been built on being available. It also, to be honest, would have been quite out of character for me. I am not good at taking a back seat; when I see something that needs doing, my inclination is to take it on. Restraining me would have been difficult. Kirk not only made no effort in that direction, however; he seemed to do the contrary. He let me take charge, often in a highly visible way, and in the most critical decisions, including, as I have reported, sometimes guidance to the trustees. Often, possibly too often, I took the initiative when I did not see it coming from him, so it could reasonably be said that any consequences for me were in substantial measure of my own doing.

The consequences of the "Kirk syndrome" of management did not involve "damage" to my career. To assert that they did would be to ignore the benefits that I enjoyed and the accomplishments to which I contributed in the years that followed the 1968 crisis. But they did result in altering my career. That cannot be denied. When I assumed the position of vice president and provost in July 1967, I expected to stay at Columbia and in that position indefinitely. Despite that expectation, however, and without any encouragement from me, my name continued to appear on various lists prepared by committees searching for presidents of colleges and universities. This had begun to happen within a few months of my becoming dean of the College in 1963, and it had occurred on a few occasions earlier, when I was chairman of the Department of Public Law and Government. After I had been dean for a few years, had experienced its frustrations, particularly in the face of evident drift and decline in the University, I gave some encouragement to these when they resulted in formal inquiries. After the 1966–67 academic year, in which I was given the responsibility I sought at Columbia, I did not encourage these inquiries. After the intense publicity surrounding the 1968 crisis, they almost disappeared. I had become too controversial.

I recall that during the summer of 1968, when I was putting out informally the word that I was interested in leaving Columbia, I had a long conversation with my old friend, John W. Gardner, in the course of which I asked him how badly my prospects had been hurt by the events at Columbia that spring. He responded candidly, "Very badly." Gardner was in a position to know because he remained close the developments in the foundation world, particularly those foundations most likely to be consulted by search committees. He was also particularly close to an institution, Stanford, then looking for a president. I had been so interested in Stanford when they offered me the position of Provost in 1966 that a sort of campaign was launched at Columbia that resulted in my declining the Stanford opportunity in favor of becoming vice president and provost at Columbia. That story is pertinent here, although it is something of a digression. (I was interviewed in 1968 by the Stanford search committee, chaired by David Packard, whom I had met when I was looked over in 1966. Perhaps out of courtesy to Gardner, I was not dropped from their list, but I got no farther than the interview.)

The appeal of Stanford essentially had been that it seemed to have just about everything that was missing at Columbia. In particular, in the person of Wallace Sterling it had a president who was active, interested, respected by his faculty, and highly effective as a fund raiser. Stanford under his leadership had become a university of the very first rank; it was definitely an institution that was "on the move." To work with Sterling, to have the opportunity to contribute to the further growth of the university, and to assist in solving some of its problems (for of course it had problems) was a challenge and a temptation that I could not ignore.

The offer from Stanford came in August, after my wife and I had made a delightful visit to Palo Alto. I at once informed Kirk and told him that I was seriously interested in the opportunity. He in turn expressed the wish that I would remain at Columbia, but characteristically he did nothing else, not even exploring the reasons for my restlessness or inquiring about what might make me decide to remain. Weeks went by essentially in silence. Stanford did not press me, but Sterling called me whenever he got to New York, which was quite often.

Finally, in October, two flattering and ultimately decisive developments occurred. The first was a memorandum dated October 27, addressed to President Kirk, and signed by 24 chairmen of departments in the arts and sciences which were represented on the College Faculty. It asked that every effort be made to dissuade me from leaving Columbia and that he meet with a group of them "to present in more detail our concern about this matter." I did not know about the memorandum, but I later was sent a copy marked, in a hand that I do not now recognize, "copy—with love." (I still do not know if the requested meeting ever was held.)

The second was an action taken by Harold F. McGuire, my very close friend on the Board of Trustees, who, when he heard rumors of my temptation by Stanford, asked me about it and about what it would take to keep me. I responded by telling him more than I previously had about my frustrations in the College deanship and about my worries over the drift and inaction at the top level. I said that the key to change was the position of provost, then held by his College classmate, Jacques Barzun. I said that in that position one might begin, even given Kirk's shortcomings, to effect changes and that I would be willing to try. What exactly he did from that point I do not know, but his efforts resulted in a letter, signed by Kirk, promising that, by the end of the 1966–67 academic year, he would arrange for Barzun to step down and for me to be made provost. (I deliberately destroyed this letter in July 1967.) Despite a somewhat uneasy feeling about the conspiratorial, almost underhanded atmosphere surrounding these arrangements, I accepted the proposition.

For present purposes the principal significance of this episode lies in illustrating Kirk's management style. He did nothing until he was pushed; he reacted but he did not lead. It also suggests that I should not have been surprised by any conduct or non-action of Kirk's after I took the position of vice president and provost. I knew what I was getting in for, at least as far as he was involved, and I had therefore forfeited any right to complain. (Why did I do it? Hubris I suppose, at least in part, but also a deep affection for Columbia and a desire to try to return it to the position of eminence that it had once occupied and for which it still, in my opinion, had the potential.)

At least until after the crisis in April 1968, Kirk and I got along extremely well. I think he meant the observation, repeatedly made, that he did not want the crisis to damage my career. The first sign of strain came early in June, when, distressed by the president's failure to give a lead to the faculty, I prepared a fairly long memorandum from my office, addressed to all members of the faculty, sketching changes in the University that needed to be made and that the crisis caused to be both urgent and possible. (In addition to my substantive proposals, I announced that I was appointing my old friend and colleague, Herbert A. Deane, Lieber Professsor of Political Philosophy, to the position of vice provost for academic planning and would ask both the president and the trustees to approve.) I gave a copy of the draft to Kirk, asked his approval for my sending it out, and said that, since I wanted to get it out without further delay, I would stay that afternoon until he could give me his reaction.

REFLECTIONS ON THE COLUMBIA DISORDERS OF 1968

Late in the day I discovered that he had left without sending me word, and I took the unusual step of calling him at home, after first ascertaining that he did not have guests. When I asked to speak to him, the word came back that he was at dinner and did not wish to be disturbed. I was so angered by that response that I at once wrote out a letter of resignation. I was determined to give it to him the first thing in the morning and to tell him that I could not forgive his action (inaction), particularly after all I had been through for the University and indeed for him. He must have realized my intention, for the next morning, in an unprecedented action, he came to my office and apologized for failing to respond to the faculty memorandum, which he thoroughly approved. I did not resign, but our relations were never quite the same after that incident.

During the summer I was away from New York more than usual. My wife, without consulting me, decided that I had to get away and booked us for a two-week trip to Bermuda and announced when we were going. Also, as we had planned, in August we made a visit to her parents in Lake Geneva, Wisconsin.

During these months I heard rumors, chiefly from friends in the faculty, of moves to persuade Kirk to resign. I did not try to verify them, and I did not discuss them with Kirk or anyone else. I was therefore not surprised by Kirk's announcement early in August of his retirement from the Columbia presidency, although he gave me no advance word of it.

Thereafter, especially during our Lake Geneva visit, which was repeatedly interrupted by telephone calls from New York, I was asked informally by members of the Board of Trustees, including the chairman, whether I would be willing to be appointed acting president. These were inquiries; they did not constitute an offer. I replied affirmatively with great reluctance, as I did to a comparable request later in the year, because I sensed that my "political capital" on the campus had been drawn down so drastically by the events of the crisis that I would be seriously handicapped in the presidency. My judgment in a sense was confirmed by the decision of the trustees to appoint Andrew Cordier, dean of the School of International Affairs, as acting president.

I go into this here because subsequent reports concerning the events of the summer have suggested that relations between Kirk and me had indeed deteriorated drastically. In particular, Courtney Brown, in his memoirs as dean of the Graduate School of Business, tells the following story. (I was inclined to accept the authenticity of the story because I knew that the Browns and the Kirks were close socially, because I could see no reason why Brown should have invented it, and because Kirk did not repudiate it when it appeared in 1983.) Brown reports:

> In mid-summer . . . [while on vacation in Maine] I had a call from Grayson Kirk asking me to return and share in the effort to prevent the trustees' appointment of David Truman, then vice president of the University and a man he had formerly sponsored, as president. I did so with a sense of urgency, feeling that, under the circumstances, his appointment would have been a mistake for Columbia and a disaster for the professional graduate schools. As a former Dean of Columbia College, he had especially resented the rule of no undergraduate classes in Uris Hall [the Graduate Business School Building]. For whatever reason, the trustees dropped his name from consideration and looked elsewhere. (Courtney C. Brown, *The Dean Meant Business*, New York: Graduate School of Business, Columbia University, 1983, p. 203)

of the late 1960s, of which the events at Columbia in 1968 are a prime example, represented severe crises. The challenges that they presented were almost invariably fundamental, defying or destroying accustomed procedures for making institutional decisions, and threatening profound, possibly devastating consequences for the university's future.

For a board of trustees to perform satisfactorily the function of crisis management, preparation is required. Its members need to know and understand the institution and its problems, and as a group they need to have worked together in a sustained fashion for a period of time sufficient to equip them collectively to meet the crisis. This means that board meetings necessarily must be occasions for acquiring and exchanging information. Actions may be unnecessary or purely formal, and for the activist, accustomed to making things happen, they may seem a bore. They need not be and they will not be if the long-term value of the information-acquiring activity is understood. In any event, it is indispensable; it is a major responsibility of the chairman and the chief executive to see that a board is a thoroughly informed group.

Douglas Knight wisely observed (Knight, p. 99) that "No board of trustees was equipped to deal with the quicksand of events of the 1960s." How well equipped was the Columbia board? In my opening chapter I asked how the Columbia trustees appeared in 1968. Even accepting, as one must, the validity of Douglas Knight's observation, it is fair to say that their performance was not impressive. Collectively they were not even equipped to handle a crisis much less severe than the one that 1968 brought. Moreover, going back only as far as the replacement of Eisenhower, the past record was not a strong one, as previously cited examples indicate. The "search" that resulted in the appointment of Grayson Kirk to the presidency was perfunctory and, at least from a faculty viewpoint, a disappointment. The handling of the Strickman filter fiasco in the summer of 1967, to cite a quite different kind of incident, was ludicrous and pathetic, if not tragic.

A more subtle example of collective incapacity is provided by the trustees' action on the College Faculty's 1966 request that the University cease sending class rankings to draft boards. This the president, as I noted in the previous chapter, finally took to the University Council in March 1967 and thence to the trustees. An informed and prudent board would have respected the faculty judgment and simply voted to affirm the action of the College Faculty and the University Council. Instead the board, possibly on the president's recommendation, took an entirely different action, voting upon what Cox reports as "purely educational grounds" to abolish altogether the calculation of class standings. (Cox, p. 45)

As a policy this may have had considerable justification, but taking it in this manner not only arrogated to the trustees a matter of educational policy, traditionally and understandably a faculty responsibility, but did so in such a way as to treat both the College Faculty and the University Council as institutions of no consequence, a treatment that did nothing to improve the already weakened credibility of the latter body. No lower court prospers from being overruled on appeal.

With respect to the events in the spring of 1968, the interesting question is why were the patterns of the trustees' actions and reactions what they were? This question is complex, and any answers are inescapably speculative, but it goes to the fundamentals of the board as an organization. It is important if one is to understand trustee purposes and limitations, indeed if the Columbia crisis itself is to be understood.

Individually, the 24 members of the board were intelligent and accomplished, many of them extremely able. They included Benjamin Buttenwieser, investment banker; William T. Gossett, general counsel of the Ford Motor Company; Frank S. Hogan, Manhattan district attorney; Arthur B. Krim, head of United Artists; Robert D. Lilley, head of AT&T; Charles F. Luce, head of the Consolidated Edison Company; Harold F. McGuire, senior member of an old New York law firm; William S. Paley, head of the Columbia Broadcasting System; Chairman William E. Petersen, head of the Irving Trust Company; Percy Uris, Manhattan real estate developer; and Lawrence A. Wien, New York lawyer and real estate investor.

Collectively, however, as I have already suggested, the trustees were unimpressive and frequently ineffectual. These judgments are severe, but they are not superficial. I knew many of the individual members well; I had worked closely with a considerable number of them for years; and I had great admiration for many of them.

A high degree of personal concern on the part of individual trustees is indicated by their conduct, as individuals, during the crisis. A number of them, how many I do not know, came up to the campus and walked about, observing and gaining direct impressions. I did not know of these visits at the time, and to my knowledge the president was also unaware of them. I attended some of their meetings when I was dean of the College and as vice president and provost I was present at all of their regular meetings. From my point of view, therefore, the behavior of the board as a collectivity in the 1968 crisis involved disappointments but few surprises.

Had I been able to, I would have worked to change the board's operating practices and other aspects of its collective behavior. I was not able to do this, of course, but in February 1969, after my resignation had been announced, I sent a confidential memorandum to a number of the trustees stating my view of the fundamental problems of the University, not the immediate consequences of the 1968 turbulence or even the serious financial problems facing the institution, but the causes underlying the decline in the University's standing over the previous two or three decades. (This memorandum was really confidential. I wrote it at home; my wife rather than my secretary typed and duplicated it; I personally mailed those that went out; and all copies were kept in my files. Some weeks after it was sent, the acting president, Andrew Cordier, said he had heard of the document and asked for a copy. I gave him one, and years later, a decade or more, I gave a copy to my closest faculty friend, the late Herbert Deane. That was it. If a copy is in the University records, it was placed there by one of the recipients, not by me.)

The memorandum covered a wide range of substantive topics in its nine single-spaced pages, most of which need not be reviewed now. It included, however, some specific comments about the board that are pertinent to the questions raised here. After arguing that the roots of Columbia's problems lay in poor management, in weak organization, and in inadequate leadership, I indicated that in my opinion the trustees could not be excluded from a share in the responsibility for these failures.

A central point in my criticisms was the board's pattern of meetings. I argued that the board met too frequently and for too short a time. Specifically, the trustees met once a month, on the first Monday afternoon, except in the summer months of June, July, August, and September, though occasional summer meetings could be held, with smaller quorum requirements, by the so-called summer committee. The regular sessions did not run the whole afternoon, however, but began about two and lasted for a couple of hours. As the two hours drew to a close, members typically began to look at their watches, and a few usually slipped out before adjournment.

This practice had several direct and indirect consequences. In the first place, a couple of hours once a month did not afford a suitable opportunity for the group to examine thoroughly any of the host of University problems. Secondly, although some of them were professional associates or active members of alumni classes, they were not the sort of closely knit group that they could have been if they met four or five times a year for at least a full day, in a setting away from the city, such as Arden House, the former Harriman estate, an hour from New York, which the University owns. Thirdly, the practice not only made the monthly meetings fairly perfunctory but also put the bulk of trustee activity into committees, especially the key groups such as finance and buildings and grounds. These made decisions between board meetings, decisions that might or might not be reported to the whole group, depending on time and inclination. Finally, committee dominance had the effect of reinforcing the parochialism of the board, all by three of whose members were New Yorkers. This was not only traditional but deliberate, as I discovered when I informally suggested that the pool from which they were selecting members was unnecessarily small and that a university with a national constituency need not, particularly in the age of jet travel, draw virtually all of its governing board from a single community. The response I got was that those at a distance would not be able to attend committee meetings!

It is interesting to note that in 1956–57 the then chairman of the board appointed a special committee, chaired by William S. Paley, "to study the role of the Trustees and to make recommendations." Its report in 1957, published as "The Role of the Trustees of Columbia University," was and is a thoughtful review, one that would have been a useful part of the initiation of a new member. It wisely observed that "Trustees are most emphatically not executives in their relation to a university." The Committee's members were attracted by the infinitives in the oath of the president of the United States prescribed in Article II of the Constitution, to "preserve, protect and defend," and they observed that trustees were looked upon as the University, "at least in time of trouble or contention." They did not explore the implications of this expectation, however. They also had no criticisms of the meeting schedule and they essentially straddled the question of parochialism in membership. Thus they said that it was "desirable that Life Trustees not be drawn too exclusively from areas close to New York City, the influences and ranges of interest of Columbia University being not only nationwide but worldwide." But they then qualified this observation by saying that "the advantages of wide geographical choice must be balanced against the availability of a candidate living at a distance from the locus of the Trustees' work, much of which is necessarily done in committee." (The Report of the

Special Trustee Committee, Adopted by the Trustees, November 4, 1957, pp. 17–20)

The ramifying effects upon the University of the board's antiquated pattern of meetings were at least two. First, it denied the top management the rhythm of administrative planning derived from meeting deadlines that occur at regular but not too frequent intervals. That rhythm is one of the elements of good management in any complex organization. At Columbia it was missing because there was always a trustee meeting impending; there were no cycles, just a continuous stream of meetings and preparations. Second, as one can easily guess, the system kept the president and his staff constantly attending committee meetings, almost without letup. Such constant meetings not only were exhausting; more seriously, they invited such committees to become involved in the sometimes trivial details of daily management in a way that did not inform the board as a whole but only confused the lines of authority within the administration.

As should be obvious, a conscientious member of the board, especially one who was assigned to an active committee, probably spent more time on Columbia matters—and with less effect—than if trustee activity had been concentrated in two-day sessions, three or four times a year.

In addition to the pattern of meetings, and related to it, was the second major deficiency that I saw in the board's performance. This was that the board was not equipped as a group to assure itself that the management's performance was of top quality by asking penetrating questions on either recurring or impending problems. In particular, it did not receive and did not insist upon receiving regular financial reports that might have given it better control and earlier warning of the University's money problems. The University should have been functioning on a three- to five-year operating and capital budget; it had instead only a clumsy and inadequate one-year operating budget put together without any adequate reports on current performance and without any reliable estimates of future income.

The trustees thus were ill equipped for the 1968 crisis or even one of smaller dimensions. A setup of the sort I have described might have worked adequately with a dominating president, like Butler. In fact, I assume that the pattern may have been a holdover from the Butler days; he may have preferred not to have a strong board, capable of questioning his authority.

From what I know, nothing or very little was done in the years immediately after 1968 to improve the pattern of board operations. Most conspicuously, the meeting schedule remained what it was. After the crisis in 1968 the campus buzzed with talk of "restructuring," and a special subcommittee of the board was set up to work with faculty and student representatives on altering structure. They replaced the University Council with a monster known as a University Senate, but apparently the board was exempt from the post crisis scrutiny. The board's membership was gradually broadened geographically, but the structure of operations remained unaltered, at least during the years when I remained in touch with the University.

During the crisis involving the building seizures the trustees met frequently, downtown rather than on the campus, since their appearance as a group on Morningside would have been a complicating factor, to say the least. Given the preparation I have described, however, their predispositions and actions, actual and proposed, were not always helpful. Their intentions were beyond criticism, but their proposals were not always appropriate, because they knew neither the University nor each other well enough to move in sure and constructive fashion.

A good example and, because of its complexity, a bad one was the handling of the issue of the gymnasium in Morningside Park. I have already said enough about this to indicate that the whole project was one of the most misunderstood undertakings any institution ever was involved in. I shall have more to say in other connections, but with respect to the trustees, the problem was whether and how to suspend or to halt construction in order to quiet the scene on the campus and in the neighborhood. The Cox Commission, in my opinion very unfairly, criticizes the hesitations of the trustees, saying that they failed to recognize that by 1968 the matter was no longer just a business transaction. (Cox, pp. 86–87) This grossly oversimplifies the problem. It is fair to say, moreover, that the late Harold F. McGuire, who among the trustees was known as "Mister Gymnasium," because he chaired the committee and because he was an enthusiast for physical education, a champion of "the duffers," was opposed to the Morningside location from the beginning. He was convinced that a contract with the City of New York would be a source of constant trouble. He was right, but though he lost the argument within the board, he continued his leadership efforts. He hesitated, along with other lawyers on the board, to drop construction because he quite reasonably feared that a breach of contract would lie against the University if they simply walked away from the construction. Hence, when suspension was announced, it was done "at the request of the mayor." Even that step was taken hesitantly, primarily because they sensed that suspension would lead to cancellation, and millions of dollars in fabricated steel was in a warehouse in New Jersey, waiting to be delivered to the site; because millions had been raised or pledged for the gym, which might have to be returned; and because no alternative site for the much-needed facility had been located.

These arguments were not laid out and faced in logical order, which meant that much of the effort at persuasion tended to skirt the center of the problem, and much of the discussion took on a fairly emotional tone. At the crucial discussion I was not present but, as I have previously noted, at President Kirk's request, I was asked to put the case to selected members of the board on the telephone. The task was neither pleasant nor easy. Some flavor of the problem is suggested by a report in the *New York Times*, quoting an interview with trustee Percy Uris, who said that he was "terribly upset" and "in many ways angry" about what was happening on the campus, and that he "would regard it as a terrible thing to abandon the gymnasium" because its construction was predicated on a "fair contract" with the city. (*New York Times*, April 27, 1968)

During the course of the crisis, some trustee actions were constructive in purpose but taken too late to be of significant value. Thus midway through the crisis week they decided that the University should retain the services of the Sydney S. Baron public relations firm. It was an organization that I had never heard of, and my impression of its representatives was that they were more suited to representing a race track than to saving the standing of a university. But that was not the point. Columbia needed a good public relations organization and had needed one for years. Appointing Sydney Baron, whatever his professional shortcomings, was a clear case of which both the president and I attended, to establish, as I have previously noted, a special subcommittee of the board. Under the chairmanship of Alan H. Temple, this subcommittee was to study restructuring and to work with the newly constituted Executive Committee of the Faculty, under Professors Westin and Sovern, on such matters. The trustees also gave legitimacy to the Westin-Sovern committee by authorizing the president to make available to it such finances as were necessary for its operations and for those of the fact-finding commission (the Cox Commission) that it proposed to appoint. The chairman of the board also volunteered that members of the Board of Trustees would be willing to testify before the Cox Commission, but to my knowledge the only one who did was Harold F. McGuire, who was chairman of the committee on the gymnasium.

These actions by the board did not mean that all was harmonious within the group. The much-debated proposal to drop the trespass charges against those who had been arrested when the buildings were cleared is an illustration. The board's problem was aggravated by the membership of the longtime district attorney of New York County, Frank Hogan, whose staff would handle the prosecutions. Hogan was decidedly a hard-liner who adamantly opposed any such action. Those of his colleagues who disagreed with his views were reluctant to oppose him, and some strongly agreed. The latter included President Kirk, who publicly stated that the trespass charges "cannot be dropped by the university." (*New York Times*, May 10, 1968) He must have known that this statement was only technically correct and that the University could ask that the trespass charges not be pressed. The board, in fact, publicly expressed the view that "the university acting alone does not have legal authority to drop trespass charges.

Such authority rests in the *prosecuting attorney* and ultimately in the court. However, the trustees accepted the view that the university can make recommendations for leniency which the court may or may not accept." (*New York Times*, May 10, 1968. Emphasis added)

I had little direct contact with the Board of Trustees after May 1968, unless I include the flurry of telephonic activity in August, principally with the chairman, over the selection of an acting president. I am, therefore, not in a position to say whether the disagreements that I observed during the crisis developed into lasting divisions.

I have the impression, however, that two distinct tendencies emerged from that period. (I use "tendencies" because they clearly were not "factions," not self-conscious groups.) One of these tendencies was a no-nonsense set who felt that police force should have been used immediately and chalked up the failure to do so to incompetence, timidity, or both. The other was a set who felt that if matters had been handled properly (though they didn't say how), it would never have been necessary to call in the police. These tendencies, which did not cover the whole board membership, were opposed to each other, of course. Nevertheless, they converged on one point. Between them they doomed any possibility that Grayson Kirk could remain as president or that my continued presence on the campus would be particularly welcome. The tar pot contained enough to smear us both.

Thus, to return to the opening questions, the Board of Trustees as crisis managers did not do well. They did not in part because the crisis was of unprecedented scale and character. But they also did not because they were not adequately equipped, as a group, to perform that difficult role effectively. Some of the fault for that deficiency was rooted in habit and history; some of it reflected the weak leadership of President Kirk; but a large share must be assigned to the members of the institution itself, who were insufficiently reflective about and thus inadequately prepared for the discharge of their central functions.

CHAPTER EIGHT

THE MAYOR AND HIS ENTOURAGE

Mayor John Lindsay early became involved in the Columbia crisis. For two reasons this was inevitable. The first and less important was that New York City's chief executives traditionally had an interest in protecting and possibly advancing the health and effectiveness of the cluster of educational and cultural institutions on Morningside Heights. This group, led by the University and including Union Theological Seminary, the Riverside Church, the Cathedral of St. John the Divine, the Juilliard School, which had not yet moved to Lincoln Center, International House and the Interchurch Center, influenced, if it did not actually determine, the quality of existence on the upper west side of Manhattan. Even in the altered circumstances of the area after World War II, it slowed the pace of change in that section of the city. Mayors varied in their understanding of the importance of this function and in their commitment to the Morningside institutions, but they could not ignore any significant threat to their operations and to their existence. The Columbia crisis in 1968 was not an exception.

The second and more important influence compelling the mayor's involvement came actively into play when the black students took over Hamilton Hall. Their action at once threatened a reaction in

Harlem and the possibility of riots. Growing militancy in the Black Power movement and opposition in the late 1960s to the previous widely accepted goals of integration were evident. Further, unrest seemed understandably to have increased after the assassination of Martin Luther King, Jr., earlier in the month. Thus the University's response to the occupation of Hamilton Hall by the black students was potentially highly explosive. In these circumstances, the last thing the mayor wanted, as one of his staff observed, was to have "a hot August in April." This concern did not diminish as various nationally known black leaders, such as H. Rap Brown, made their appearance on the campus. Early in the crisis, therefore, word reached the principal University officers that the city authorities were afraid of the possibility that if we proceeded against the occupants of Hamilton Hall, we would provoke an outbreak of rioting in Harlem. This was a fear that we felt, of course, well before the word came from City Hall.

But the Mayor had been drawn into the controversy, had indeed been made a party to it, as far back as December 1965 by the actions of his parks commissioner, Thomas P. Hoving. These actions added up to a public attack on the Columbia gymnasium project in Morningside Park, although it was going forward under a lease with the parks department that had been authorized by the governor, the state legislature, and the legislative and executive authorities of the city, including Hoving's two predecessors as parks commissioner, Robert Moses and Newbold Morris.

The Cox Commission report (pp. 76–89) gives an essentially accurate account of the project and the controversy that developed around it. When, however, it asserts that "the opposition was not generated by Commissioner Hoving," it is being politically naïve and unaccountably ignorant of the history of the enterprise and of the realities of life in Morningside Park.

The project dated back to 1960 and was a logical outgrowth of a highly successful collaboration between the University and the community (including the parks department) on the construction and operation of a baseball diamond and playing field at the south end of the park. For several years this had been used during the school year and on weekdays by Columbia and on weekends and in the summer by community teams organized and coached by Columbia staff at the University's expense. The playing field project meant that that part of the park was reclaimed from the gangs and the junkies who made the rest of it an area that residents of the community, black or white, entered only at their peril.

Several black groups from Harlem supported the gymnasium lease when it was pending before the city council. More significant, the bill authorizing the lease was introduced in the state legislature by Senator James L. Watson of West Harlem, an eloquent and vigorous black civil rights leader, and among those who voted for it was Percy Sutton, then a black member of the state assembly and by 1968 Manhattan borough president.

In the 1965 campaign for mayor, the Lindsay organization issued a white paper concerning the parks, written by Hoving, that in passing criticized the Morningside Park lease. The matter might have stopped there, but Hoving in December 1965, now speaking as parks commissioner, publicly attacked the gymnasium lease on the grounds of the impropriety of using public parkland for private purposes. (The first public attack by Hoving produced a typically clumsy effort at response by the University. Wesley First, who then and temporarily was handling public relations, could get no one in the president's office to respond. Instead he was obliged to call on me, a relatively invisible dean of the College, to denounce Hoving's action. This I did, of course, before the television cameras, but it was hardly a contest between equals.)

What the Hoving offensive amounted to in political terms was that a Republican white parks commissioner, acting for a recently elected white Republican mayor, who incidentally had achieved considerable popularity in Harlem, appeared ahead and on the left of Harlem's Democratic black leadership. Hoving's action thus gave prominence to the gymnasium matter, as he intended. It also had the possibly unintended effect of making it a partisan and a racial issue. The University was a favorite target of many demagogues. For it to be attacked successfully in the name of the community by a white politician and a Republican was an intolerable affront and challenge to the black Democratic leadership of Harlem. Small wonder then that in early 1966 a bill to repeal the 1960 enabling legislation was introduced in the state legislature by Senator Basil Patterson of Harlem and Assemblyman Percy Sutton. The bill did not go anywhere, and it probably was not intended to. Rather it was to serve as an instrument of coercion, even of blackmail, as I shall indicate later.

Hoving's hypocrisy, even duplicity, is revealed in two settings. First, he met with President Kirk and trustee McGuire, plus the gymnasium's architect, in January of 1966. But in this meeting he did not argue on the principled grounds that public parks should not be used for private purposes, which he had used in his public pronouncements. Rather he objected only to the detailed *terms* of the lease: the rental and the division of space between the University and the community. Second, a year later he resigned as parks commissioner to become director of the Metropolitan Museum of Art. In that capacity he took an untroubled lead in a successful drive to appropriate a large additional chunk of Central Park for a proposed large addition to the museum. This was perhaps just an illustration of the classic political proposition that where you stand depends upon where you sit, but it was still a clear about-face and must have required considerable Jesuitical agility.

The introduction of the Patterson-Sutton repeal bill was followed, over an extended period in 1966 and 1967 by a long series of meetings. This series was far more extensive and much more focused than the Cox Commission report suggests (pp. 80-81). I attended most of these meetings, along with various trustees, notably Harold McGuire. The president attended some of them and, during 1966 and early 1967, Lawrence Chamberlain, then the vice president of the University, was a participant. All of the Harlem Democratic leadership were present, including Patterson, Sutton, and Assemblyman Charles Rangel, Sutton's successor after he became Manhattan borough president. Several of the meetings were held in the mayor's residence, Gracie Mansion, and Mr. Lindsay was regularly present, as a moderator rather than an active negotiator. The parks commissioner was never present.

The significance of these meetings lies not only in their being held over an extended period, but in the purposes and tactics of the Harlem politicians. There was essentially no talk of the alleged impropriety of the use of parkland for private purposes or of the possibility of canceling the lease. From the outset it was clear that what the Harlem leaders wanted was a recognizably better deal for the community. They knew that the existence of a community gymnasium in the park, with activities going on in the daytime and in the evenings, when lights would be on in that whole south section of the park, would contribute significantly to the area's security. They saw the value in extending on an all-year basis the advantages, for the community and for its young men, of the playing field activity. They also knew that the city would not build any such facility. Consequently their first proposal, one to which they constantly returned, was that the entire gymnasium structure be shared between the University and the community. This would not only provide the community with a better facility, but it would also get rid of the unfortunate Jim Crow symbolism of the (white) University gymnasium on top and the (black) community structure on the bottom.

This proposal was seriously and intensively discussed by the University officials between meetings of the whole group. When it became obvious that such a sharing arrangement would prove to be wholly unworkable, that conclusion was reported to the Harlem leaders and the difficulties explained. Various alternatives were explored; ones that would still involve separate community and University facilities but would be designed to get rid of the Jim Crow problem. The architect was asked several times to draft new designs along these lines. None of these efforts proved successful.

Finally, the University tried to help with the problem of the Harlem political leadership by offering to increase substantially the community portion of the gymnasium by the addition of a swimming pool and to provide for its operation and staffing. This was accepted by the politicians, though obviously with less than total enthusiasm, and Percy Sutton as borough president agreed to sponsor in the Board of Estimate the necessary legislation modifying the lease.

The Harlem politicians had made a good try and, but for the disruption on the Columbia campus, they might have succeeded. But they could not control events in the University, and they could not stifle loud and conspicuous objections from potentially rival elements in the area. These were reinforced by the presence of increasingly militant elements in the black community, and they were given ample opportunity to develop effectiveness by the slowness of the University in raising the necessary funds for the gymnasium. Such structures are notoriously difficult to finance through private contributions, so the eight-year gap between authorization and the beginning of construction was not remarkable. It was unfortunate, however, in that it coincided with a marked change in the political climate within the Harlem community. The precipitating influence for all of these negative factors, however, was the action of Parks Commissioner Hoving.

Mayor Lindsay acknowledged his involvement in the Columbia crisis soon after the first building was taken over. In the early morning of April 24, or possibly April 25, he telephoned me at my apartment. He told me he thought I should understand that if he were asked to mediate in the situation, he would have to take into account the whole situation, including the gymnasium, and not just the building seizures. I thanked him for his call and for his concern and told him that we did not then propose his mediation. In fact, we never considered asking him to mediate, though in hindsight it might have been a constructive move. At a later stage members of the Ad Hoc motion the actions planned previously with the high command of the police department. At the time he called, the police were already assembling, approximately a thousand of them, and we responded, without any deliberation, that the thing had gone too far to be called off.

I do not know what precipitated the mayor's action or who, if anyone did, persuaded him to take it. I do know that just before the police action on April 29-30, the mayor telephoned a Columbia alumnus and told him that the action was on. This friend, Judge Charles Metzner, who is also a friend of mine, recently told me that Mayor Lindsay feared that, because the police were not properly trained to handle a situation such as ours, there might be bloodshed, perhaps on a considerable scale. As I have noted, the Ad Hoc Faculty Group made some sort of effort to persuade both the governor and the mayor to intervene. I do not know if they reached Mr. Rockefeller, but the mayor's office stated that he had never received any such request (*New York Times*, April 30, 1968). The *New York Times* reported that on Sunday, April 28, "Manhattan Borough President Percy Sutton, several members of the State Legislature, City Councilman Theodore Weiss [a Reform Democrat], and a number of Democratic district leaders" in a telegram urged the mayor "to keep the police from ejecting the students from the campus buildings they occupied." The reported reasons were that forcible ejection of the students could "only cause violence on the campus and clearly increase tensions in the surrounding community." (*New York Times*, April 29, 1968)

The mayor's was not the only last-minute request that we received. As reported in chapter 5, at an equally late hour on the night of April 29–30, Kenneth Clark and Theodore Kheel asked us to call off the police action. We were grateful for the efforts that these two men had made, especially with the students in Hamilton Hall, and we did not want to offend them. Nevertheless we felt obliged to tell them that we could not accept their request. This is a point that the Cox Commission does not mention. (Cox, pp. 133–35)

Should we have acceded to these appeals? I regret to say that I do not think so. The very idea of such a police action is and was abhorrent. But what would have been gained by further delay? There was absolutely no evidence and no prospect of a willingness to compromise by the leaders of either the SDS or the black students, who in fact seemed to be playing a sort of game of chicken with each other, neither being willing to yield before the other. Calling off the action, therefore, would have meant only a further delay and in a situation that was deteriorating. Had we been ready to grant complete amnesty, which even the Ad Hoc Faculty Group's leadership opposed, we would likely have gained only time until the SDS activists seized upon another "issue" to produce another confrontation. And amnesty would likely have been seen as a betrayal by the large majority of students who were not SDS sympathizers. We were, of course, already being sharply criticized for not calling in the police. Should we sanction the police action, we knew that we would be, and of course were, accused of brutality and barbaric lack of sympathy with the students. But I do not think that we had a reasonable alternative.

I suspect that privately the mayor would have agreed, had he been asked. Certainly, aside from his last-minute telephone call, he made no comment that could be regarded as criticizing our decision. (He did, as I shall indicate in the next chapter, request an inquiry into whether the police had used unreasonable force, an action which he really was formally obliged to take.) In fact, in a speech in the Middle West immediately after the police action he said that the performance of the Columbia officials was "a remarkable display of patience and restraint." He also said that the students who had seized the University buildings had "clearly exceeded even the most liberal perimeters of the right to assemble and dissent." (*New York Times*, April 30, 1968)

The mayor could not avoid being involved in the Columbia crisis. His involvement, however, on balance was neither improper nor unconstructive. He had substantial official and political stakes in the situation, which he handled with courage and decency.

CHAPTER NINE

BLACK POLITICIANS ON THE SPOT

I have discussed in the preceding chapter the awkward challenge to the (Democratic) black political leadership of Harlem presented by the attack by parks commissioner Hoving on the project for the Columbia community gymnasium in Morningside Park. I also touched on the threat to these politicians from the changing dynamics of the civil-rights/black-power movement. Nevertheless something further needs to be said about the part that these black politicians played in the Columbia crisis and about the circumstances in which they found themselves.

In looking at these leaders it is important to bear in mind that the decade of the 1960s marked a fundamental change in the character of the politics of communities like Harlem. Symbolized in the shift of preferred labels from "Negro" to "Black," the change was toward increased militancy and a growing tendency to move away from accommodation to the white power structure and toward confrontation and more insistent demands. Moreover, although the leadership of Martin Luther King, Jr. emphasized nonviolence along with militancy, the likelihood of violence occurring in any crisis was increasingly strong. The commitment to nonviolence in the movement for black power was not uniform, and the resulting tension meant that mainstream leaders were constantly subject to becoming outmoded because they were insufficiently insistent on changes in the treatment of the black community and changes in the experiences of its individual members.

This new and rather fluid situation meant that the established leaders in Harlem no longer have a quasi-monopoly on the role of spokesmen for the black community. To some degree goaded by those of their number who were more militant, such as state senator Basil Patterson, they were obliged to share the spotlight with new actors whose power bases were not in the old and recognized political structures but in more popular and more unconventional organizations and movements. For example, on the second evening of the crisis, April 24, a press conference was held, not at one of the political clubs, but at the Harlem branch of the Congress of Racial Equality, better known under the acronym of CORE. It was addressed by Percy Sutton, who spoke about a meeting, to be discussed shortly, with University officials earlier in the day. But the platform for this "old guard" representative was shared with Victor Solomon, chairman of Harlem CORE, with Omar Ahmed, vice chairman of the National Conference of Black Power, and with other activists who were not yet elected government officials. (*New York Times*, April 25, 1968)

This was the context in which a meeting was held on the afternoon of April 24 with President Kirk and me. It was attended by Manhattan borough president Percy Sutton, state senator Basil Patterson, assemblyman Charles Rangel, William Booth, chairman of the Human Rights Commission of the City, and Barry Gottehrer, the mayor's assistant.

BLACK POLITICIANS ON THE SPOT

At whose initiative the meeting was held I do not recall, but its urgency was caused by the black students (and members of the Harlem community) having taken over Hamilton Hall from the white students, whom they had forced to leave the building in the early hours of April 24. The discussion at the meeting was exclusively concerned with working out a proposal to those occupying Hamilton Hall that would persuade them freely to evacuate the building. The result was an offer to the black students that, if they would leave the building, giving their names, and would accept disciplinary probation for a year, the University would agree to take no punitive actions against them under the criminal law, either for trespass or for holding hostage the dean of the College, and the president would further agree to call a meeting of the trustees to consider suspending and revising the gymnasium project.

Sutton, accompanied by Patterson and Rangel, agreed to convey this proposal to the Hamilton occupants. Cox (p. 113) reports that they did deliver this message, but he cites no evidence that they did, and at a later point in his report (p. 144) he says, "Some participants [in the meeting] thought that they [the proposals] were to be put before the students by borough president Sutton and there may have been misunderstanding about the presentation." These contradictory statements tend to support my conviction that Sutton never delivered the message but rather suggested to the students that they sit tight. His later public statements about the meeting with President Kirk omit any reference to such a message, as I shall indicate later. Further, we never heard anything back from the Sutton group and there is no evidence that any such message affected the behavior of the Hamilton Hall students in subsequent days. In fact, statements by black student leaders after the police action on April 30 indicate that they were determined to be arrested but had decided on their own not to resist arrest, and during the occupation had drills on how they would respond when the police arrived. (*New York Times*, May 2, 1968)

In any event, the essence of the proposal to Sutton was later in the day put into a letter from Alexander Platt, associate dean of the College, to the Hamilton Hall students. In response to objections that Platt could not commit the University, his letter was supplemented by one from President Kirk endorsing Platt's statements. The letter signed by Kirk also added a promise to recommend favorably to the trustees a College Faculty resolution proposing a review of the gymnasium project with a group from the community to be designated by the mayor and asking that work on the project be suspended.

Whether or not Sutton and his colleagues sabotaged our efforts to negotiate with the Hamilton Hall occupants, it is obvious to me now that these attempts marked a turning point in the whole crisis. We, of course, genuinely sought a peaceful, negotiated evacuation for its own sake. But it is clear now that had our attempts been successful, at that point—before the seizure of any additional buildings other than Hamilton and the president's office in Low Library—the crisis would have been over. As Cox observes (p. 145), if the proposals had been accepted in Hamilton, their essential terms would almost certainly have been extended to other students. This probability highlights the critical role of the black politicians in the whole affair and emphasizes the elements of tragedy in the story. There were other turning points, notably the one at which the leaders of the Ad Hoc Faculty Group betrayed their University, but none by hindsight had the same almost inexorable consequences.

The awkward, essentially defensive position of the black politicians is evident in the highly selective recall of events and actions involving them, during the crisis. For example, at the press conference on the evening of April 24, mentioned above, the reports indicated that Sutton, talking about the meeting earlier in the day that he and his colleagues had held with University officials, made no mention of the central concern of the meeting. He said nothing about the long discussion and about its focus on persuading the black students in Hamilton to evacuate the building peaceably. Rather he said that he and his colleagues had met with Kirk "to make the university aware of potential danger in the anger of the Harlem community." (*New York Times*, April 25, 1968) Of course, "the university" needed no such warning. That threat accordingly was never explicitly discussed at the meeting. The closest Sutton came to reporting what actually took place was his statement that Kirk had agreed to call a meeting of the Board of Trustees to reconsider the gymnasium project. There was no mention of an offer to the black students, no reference to a visit by the Sutton group to Hamilton Hall, and no reference to what was the central focus of the whole meeting.

After the police action on April 29–30, Sutton returned to essentially the same theme, talking about "his" meeting with Kirk on April 24. On May 1 he said that in that meeting he had "urged Columbia officials to relocate their [gymnasium] project." He added that on that day Kirk had told him that interruption of the construction contract would make the University liable for $5 million. The response: "I said, 'Are you telling me your investment of money is more important than possible lives if a conflagration began?'" Sutton was reported to have added that Harlem resentment was as inflamed as Newark sentiment over a projected medical center that preceded the previous summer's rioting. The response he received, in his words, was "Columbia's attitude was 'the public be damned.'" (*New York Times*, May 2, 1968) If any such interchange occurred in the April 24 meeting, I did not hear it. Sutton made no observation proposing the relocation of the gymnasium; no discussion occurred concerning the cost of withdrawing from the contract; and there were no comparative references to the 1967 Newark riots. What Sutton reported, moreover, was so at variance with the purpose of the meeting and with the written results, in the form of the Platt and Kirk letters, that one cannot escape the conclusion that Sutton's statements were crafted for the meeting that he was later addressing. Either his recollections were hopelessly faulty, which seems unlikely, or he simply invented a story for his own political purposes, which is both likely and understandable.

After the April 29–30 police action, I received other indications of selective recall by black politicians and others. In the long interview that I did over Channel 13 on May 3, 1968, with students from the School of Journalism, I reported on the discussions that we had held in 1966 and 1967, noted in the preceding chapter. I stated that once and only once during these negotiations had someone suggested that we cancel the gymnasium project. This produced immediate objections from all the others present. To this one of the student reporters said that she had talked with Rangel, Patterson, and others and had been told that they favored a complete halt in the construction project.

BLACK POLITICIANS ON THE SPOT

The belligerent tone of Sutton's remarks did not disappear in later weeks, but it was early succeeded by comments of a much more relaxed, more conciliatory quality. Thus assemblyman Charles B. Rangel, in an interview a few days later, was quoted as saying, "I believe that at long last the university has been made aware that [it is] a member of a much larger community." (*New York Times*, May 5, 1968)

In our worried concern over the possibility of igniting a riot in Harlem and therefore our desperate desire to achieve an early and peaceful accommodation with the black students in Hamilton Hall, we turned to the city's leading black politicians. We could not help hoping that they would be willing and able to assist us in finding a solution. We were improvising where there were no precedents and under conditions that gave few grounds for hope, but we had to try and to trust, tentatively, even though our judgments gave us little encouragement. We hoped that the black politicians—Sutton, Patterson, and Rangel—would assist with a solution, although we had every reason to expect that they were merely part of the problem, as sadly they indeed were.

CHAPTER TEN
THE POLICE: PRO AND CON

As I have already testified, the summoning of the police to clear the occupied buildings was the most painful decision, by the administration and faculty the most dreaded possibility, and probably for everyone the most remembered event in the Columbia crisis of 1968. Controversy surrounds every aspect of the issue of police intervention and at almost every point in its evolution.

Perhaps, as many have argued, the error lay not in summoning the police but in not doing so that first afternoon, when President Kirk proposed doing so and I resisted the idea. I still think I was not wrong. I never wanted to call the police. To use force to settle an issue, any issue, was at variance with my deep personal and professional convictions. Except as a very last resort, the police should have no part in managing a university.

Even some of those who are highly critical of the course that the administration of the University followed in the troubled times leading to and during the crisis share that view. Thus those who have argued that the crisis was aggravated because in dealing with incidents leading to the April 23 eruption, crime was not treated as crime, acknowledge "a generally accepted though tacit assumption that application of the criminal law is inappropriate in dealing with large-scale deviant behavior on a university campus." (Lusky and Lusky, p. 209) It was assumed to be inappropriate not for tactical considerations but because it violated fundamental conceptions of the institution. A university is a largely self-governing community, founded on trust and functioning with a high degree of collegiality and a minimum of hierarchy. It is not merely a community devoted to reason and civility but one in which those attributes are essential to its existence.

Small wonder that in normal circumstances the campus was patrolled by a handful of unarmed security guards whose primary functions were to enforce parking regulations and to see that the buildings were locked at the appropriate hours. Prior to April 1968, the only recorded exception to the practice of not using the city police was in connection with the disruption of the Naval ROTC ceremony in May 1965, when a handful of police were called in by the director of campus security to assist the campus guards. They did little more than augment the university patrol.

When, therefore, the Cox Commission says that by midweek of the crisis "the University officials seem to have felt that the only solution would prove to be calling the police," it is essentially correct. But it is also right when it observes that "the Administration never closed its mind to peaceful solutions." (Cox, p. 115) We shared the general abhorrence of police on the campus.

We were not only reluctant to put the matter in the hands of the police; we were also inexperienced, even naïve in such matters. We did, however, early in the crisis consult with a group of top police officials, including Assistant Chief Inspector Eldridge Waithe and Deputy Chief Inspector James Taylor, plus Commissioner William

Booth, who was chairman of the Human Rights Commission, and Barry Gottehrer, the mayor's assistant. This conference took place on Wednesday morning, April 24, in the improvised president's quarters on the ground floor of Low Library.

The burden of this conversation was whether to attempt one of several devices for freeing Dean Coleman, who was being held hostage in Hamilton. None of these was conceived to be either safe or effective. It was agreed almost at once that an assault on the building in an effort to clear it not only would put Coleman in greater danger but almost inevitably would risk provoking an uprising in Harlem. That having been agreed to, a crucial question, really a request, was put to the police officers: Would they clear the students who were occupying the president's suite in Low but not make any gesture towards those in Hamilton? The answer, as clear in my memory as if it had been given five minutes ago, was no; the police could no clear one building without going into both of those then occupied.

This is one of the pivotal incidents of the entire encounter, one on which recollections apparently differ and one whose handling has produced considerable criticism of the administration. The chief divergence in recollections is reported as follows by Cox:

> Focusing upon Low Library exclusively, this was clearly the moment to use the police to evict the remaining students if there was ever to be police intervention.
>
> Dr. Truman testified that the University officials broached this question but were told that the police could not clear Low Library without also moving against Hamilton Hall . . .
>
> Inspector Waithe's recollection is somewhat different. A sergeant who had walked through

> President Kirk's suite early Wednesday morning advised him that the students could probably be removed with little difficulty. Inspector Waithe discussed this possibility with University officials but was told that the University did not want the police to forcibly remove the students because it might be possible to persuade them to leave voluntarily. (p. 160)

I cannot quarrel with the Cox Commission's conclusion that they had "no basis for preferring one man's recollection over the other" (p. 160), but I cannot accept it. In the first place, Cox acknowledges in a later passage that Waithe recalls the conversation that I remember and have reported above but says his notes indicate that it took place at a later time. He does not, however, change the response that I recall. Second, for us at that point to have declined to clear the President's suite would have been inconsistent with all that we were attempting. Our concerns were Hamilton Hall and Harlem; to have cleared Low would have been to isolate the situation in Hamilton and to focus entirely upon it. We had no reason to want to rely entirely upon persuasion in connection with Low or to have confidence that it would be effective.

A more serious criticism is the Luskys' (Lusky and Lusky, p. 211) that we should have appealed to a higher level of authority the police decision not to clear one building without doing both. They are right that we would have "at least . . . put the city authorities to the necessity of justifying the weird position in public." (And they are also right (pp. 216–217) that the cost of not moving against either building at that point was much higher because failure to move facilitated the blossoming of rebellion in other segments of the

THE POLICE: PRO AND CON

campus community not related to the SDS or the black students' organization, SAS.)

This, of course, is hindsight, a critique of an incident that displays the risks of misunderstanding, the errors to which quick judgments may lead, and, I think one can say without indulging in hyperbole, one that underscores the essential tragedy of the situation.

Although intermittent contact with the police continued over the next two days, the next event came late Thursday night after Avery, Fayerweather, and finally Mathematics had been seized. The president then concluded that the situation was entirely out of hand and notified the police that the University wanted their help to clear the buildings. It was then that I asked his permission to carry his decision to the group of faculty meeting in Philosophy Hall, which I did, as I have reported in an earlier chapter. Cox is undoubtedly right when he says my "manner was curt." He is assuredly right in describing me as "Tired by strain, lack of sleep, and conflicting emotions." (Cox, p. 118)

The ensuing stampede by members of the faculty group to the one ground-floor entrance of Low coincided with the arrival, in plain clothes, of a unit of police to participate in making plans for clearing the buildings. As they forced their way in, the ensuing scuffle resulted in a bloody but minor head injury to Richard Greeman, a junior member of the French department. Partly because of this and largely because of a plea from some representatives of the Ad Hoc Faculty Group, I was allowed to make the announcement, as I have earlier reported, that the request for police assistance had been postponed and that "at the request of the mayor" construction on the gymnasium had been suspended.

REFLECTIONS ON THE COLUMBIA DISORDERS OF 1968

It was well that this police action was aborted, for it was at once evident that a great deal of time was going to be necessary for planning a police action on such a scale, if it were to be effective and if serious injury were to be avoided or minimized. The price of the decision, of course, was that we could not call in the police again before Monday night. A huge peace rally was scheduled for Central Park on Saturday, which would make it impossible for the department to mobilize a force of the size necessary to clear the five buildings until the rally and any aftermath were things of the past. No aftermath of any consequence developed, but the police had a fortunately unfounded apprehension that the rally might adjourn and march up Broadway to Columbia. (Another, less obvious price of the delay was the one that we had been paying since April 23: The longer a police action was postponed, the more the building occupation came, on the campus, to seem normal.)

Press accounts of the police action, when it came on the night of April 29–30, may not reveal the fact, but the truth is that much of the next four days was devoted, by police representatives and by various members of the University staff, to working out detailed plans for the police to evacuate the buildings. I did not participate in all of these. I had other responsibilities, including making the arrangements for the meeting on Sunday morning of the Columbia Faculties on Morningside Heights, the improvised faculty legislative body that met in the auditorium of the Law School. But I sat in on enough of the meetings with the police to know that the plans were made carefully, that every emphasis was placed on keeping injuries to a minimum. We did not fear the consequences of a lack of police training in handling such a campus crisis, a fear, as I reported in an earlier chapter, which troubled Mayor Lindsay. But we tried to cover every other contingency.

The plans devoted much time to exploring where possible access to the buildings could be had from the heat tunnels. This route would avoid, where such access could be had, the need for a direct assault on the buildings from the outside. (As it turned out, only Low and Hamilton could be reached via the tunnels.) It was understood that occupants who left the buildings voluntarily and peaceably would not be arrested. Although amnesty had not been granted, arrest was reserved for those who resisted. In that connection, we learned that two civil rights lawyers were with the black students in Hamilton Hall. We requested that these men not be arrested or interfered with in any way, and this was followed. It was also agreed that patrol wagons for transporting arrested persons would not be brought onto the campus, but would be parked on the periphery in order to reduce confusion and the likelihood of injury to bystanders who were merely curious. Thus we asked that only uniformed police be used. We also asked for reassurance that the police would be accompanied by medical personnel and ambulances. Not all of these arrangements were adhered to, but we tried to plan as carefully as we could.

Although the police wanted to have the action in the early hours of the morning, when they expected the numbers of the curious to be small, we knew our constituency well enough to know that for many of them night would become day and few would go to bed and miss the show.

When the police action came, it was even more traumatic than I expected. I did not directly witness it, because the president and I had been told that for our own safety we should not be on the campus. I have some feeling that I should have ignored that advice. Of course, I could not have done anything on the outside, but I could have been a witness and could thus have been better prepared to know what, if anything, went wrong. As it was, I could hear the turmoil and I received reports from various staff people who were witnesses.

In view of what might have happened, it is not unreasonable to say that nothing went wrong. In particular, as I have already noted, the evacuation of Hamilton Hall was orderly and professional, as the black students conducted themselves with dignity and self-discipline. But the operation was inherently messy, and some aspects of the operation were not anticipated. That was inevitable, as detailed tactics were devised on the spot and had to be. When one calls in the fire department, one cannot say, "Do not get water on Mother's grand piano."

Tactical considerations led those in command to bring the police vans onto the campus rather than keep them on the periphery, which concentrated the confusion. The resistance in and especially outside some of the buildings, notably Fayerweather and Mathematics, was far greater than anticipated. In consequence the arrests, more than 700, were much more numerous than expected. And there were some injuries, according to press reports, 148. (*New York Times*, May 6, 1968) These were mostly flesh wounds from police night sticks, which produced more blood than pain and made spectacular photographs for the newspapers and for the posters that appeared on the campus a day or so later. But the remarkable thing was that the injuries were few and, except in the case of one policeman who suffered a heart attack and another whose back was hurt badly, they were minor. Apparently some medical personnel, from Cornell, Mt.

THE POLICE: PRO AND CON

Sinai Hospital, New York University, and elsewhere, who for unaccountable reasons were in the buildings, were in some instances roughed up and were prevented from giving first aid. Since treatment of the injured was, by law and by agreement, a police responsibility, and since these medical persons had not been asked to assist, their complaints cannot be regarded as a miscarriage of plans, however regrettable the incidents involving them.

Many of the police disliked what they had to do. One sergeant was quoted as saying, "The truth is that a few guys let off some steam, but basically we were doing a job, a nasty job, and there's just no way to do it without someone getting hurt." (*New York Post*, May 3, 1968) Nevertheless, enough complaining of police brutality or unnecessary force appeared in the press so that Mayor Lindsay directed the police commissioner, Howard R. Leary, to investigate and report. Lindsay later said that "independent reports" persuaded him that some policemen used "excessive force." (*New York Times*, May 3, 1968) The police report indicated that some injuries occurred among those who resisted arrest, and it acknowledged that it may have been a mistake to use a number of non-uniformed officers for "operational" rather than merely "investigative" purposes, a procedure that had been criticized by the building occupants and their sympathizers. The report emphasized, however, that in some of the buildings occupants hurled furniture, bottles, and other objects at police, that physical attacks on police were "on a large scale," and that in such circumstances the police were obliged to meet force with force. (*New York Times*, May 7, 1968)

I had and have no way of checking any of these claims, but I went into three of the buildings, Fayerweather, Low Library, and

Mathematics, shortly after the police action, and I can testify that the damage to furnishings, walls, and floors was such that it was clear that violent resistance had been planned and carried out by the occupants. The police may in some instances have used avoidable force, but they do not do that kind of damage.

The two subsequent police actions during the 1968 weeks of crisis were generally more, but in certain respects were less, orderly and professional than the first. These were the evacuation of the apartment house on 114th Street on May 17 and the clearing of Hamilton Hall and the campus on the night of May 21–22. In the first of these, as I have reported in a previous chapter, the police at about 4 a.m. cleared the building without violence. Of the 117 persons reported to have been arrested, 56 were identified as Columbia students. (Cox, p. 170)

The May 21–22 action was precipitated by a defiance of the College dean's efforts to enforce the disciplinary procedures adopted by the Joint Committee of Discipline in connection with the first "bust." It was led by Mark Rudd, who was arrested on the complaint, amusingly enough, of an undercover officer who had penetrated the SDS ranks and who could charge Rudd with inciting to riot, encouraging others to resist arrest forcibly, destroying furniture and fixtures in the building, and setting a fire in Hamilton. Despite Rudd's efforts, the evacuation was carried out without violence. This again, as in the April 30 action, was in part because the police entered Hamilton from the heat tunnels and were able in effect to take the occupants from behind.

The disorderly and admittedly violent part of that night's action came after the evacuation of Hamilton when, in response to rioting

THE POLICE: PRO AND CON

and destruction on the campus—notably the breaking of large windows in Low Library and the setting of a fire in Fayerweather—the president requested the police to clear the campus. It was then that the excessive force and unnecessary police violence occurred at the hands of at least some of the officers present. Some not only cleared the open campus but also pursued retreating students into the dormitories. Numerous injuries were inflicted, none of them serious but all of them unwarranted and unnecessary. The worst consequence of these actions, and a serious one, was that the tensions and hostilities on the campus were revived and strengthened.

I can understand why the president called for clearing the campus, although he was given contrary advice by the associate dean of the College, Alexander Platt, who, as I have reported in chapter 6, had reason to believe that the crowd on the campus would quiet down once the arrested demonstrators had been removed. Kirk understandably if inaccurately felt that damage to the buildings and their contents at the hands of rioters was imminent and unacceptable. I did not attempt to dissuade the president from his decision to have the police clear the campus. I wish I had. Platt, I am sure, was right.

Police were again on the campus on June 4. They were in and around the Cathedral of St. John the Divine, in plain clothes and in uniform, to see that the Commencement ceremonies were not disrupted. They were not, despite a walkout staged at the beginning of the proceedings by a group of Columbia College students, joined according to some accounts by a few members of the teaching staff. (*New York Times*, June 5, 1968) Since this action had been anticipated, the College contingent had been seated at the extreme west end of the huge nave, far from the chancel, where the focus of that, after the spring storms were over, a group of *Spectator* editors put out in book form an account of the crisis that was generally quite accurate in its reports though partial toward the demonstrators in its judgments. Avorn, et al., *Up Against the Ivy Wall*, New York, Atheneum, 1968)

The important point about the two student enterprises is not how objective they were in their reporting but rather that they were essentially the only means of communication within the University community. They were relied upon by the administration because we had no alternative available to us.

A University newsletter, which appeared occasionally, was not suitable for informing the campus and interested "outsiders" about what was going on, from the point of view, of course, of the administration. Faculty and others thus were obligated to rely on the student radio and newspaper for their information or upon the metropolitan media. An attempt to compensate for this deficiency was one of the reasons for our improvising the meeting of the Columbia Faculties on Morningside Heights on Sunday, April 28. It was one way, admittedly awkward, of communicating directly with as many as possible of the faculty most directly affected concerning what had occurred and what was being attempted by the administration.

Reliance upon the student and the metropolitan media thus reflected a real communications gap in the University. Evident primarily in a crisis such as that in April 1968, it resulted from the existence in an earlier and simpler day of a genuine university community in which informal channels of communication were adequate to meet the needs of the institution and its members. That sort of arrangement had a civilized quality, a sort of dignified charm that made the academic community in quieter days attractive and livable. In times of crisis in which the assumptions underlying the community were being attacked, the communications gap and the forced reliance upon the student media and the metropolitan media were a menacing danger.

The New York press, television, and radio were present in force throughout the crisis, and events at Columbia soon became national news. This was an inevitable consequence of the University's location in the information center of the United States. Home of the country's only national newspaper, the *New York Times*, of the principal wire services, of the radio and television networks, and of the national news magazines, New York produced or at least processed the bulk of the nation's news. What happened at a New York institution, therefore, did not remain local. This was the price of Columbia's location. If the same event had taken place in Princeton, New Haven, or Cambridge, it would not have had the same instantaneous and intensive news treatment.

The Columbia crisis received plenty of national attention. The *New York Times* had a substantial staff on the campus, including on April 29–30, the day of the first police action, the managing editor, A. M. Rosenthal. The television and radio networks and their local affiliates were continuously present. *Newsweek, Time*, and their counterparts had reporters on the campus regularly. The result was a volume and intensity of coverage comparable to that received by a political event of major national importance. Months later I was told by a network news executive that when they reviewed, at the end of 1968, the stories that had received the most attention in their transmissions, the Columbia crisis turned out to be one of the three or magazine, "The student rebels are all tactics and no principles. We're all principles and no tactics." (Keller, *Columbia College Today*, Spring, 1968, p. 30)

As I have previously indicated, the president and I held a few press conferences, jointly or individually, but these were not sufficient to meet the need. At the very least to respond to the queries of members of the press, someone needed to be readily accessible who could speak for the University. The press office and its director could not do this, since no one in that group was close enough to the center of things. They could prepare and release what they were given, but that was about all that they were equipped or expected to do.

Gradually recognizing this situation, the president informally designated George Fraenkel, dean of the Graduate Faculties, as press spokesman. Fraenkel was involved in discussions and negotiations from the start of the demonstrations, and his office suite had been taken over by the president as a headquarters after his own office was occupied by the protestors. Fraenkel had the standing and the familiarity with policy to permit him to respond satisfactorily to the demands of the reporters.

This kind of improvising would have been unnecessary, of course, if the University and especially the president had had a public relations officer. Recognition of this need led members of the trustees, which ones I do not know, to retain the services of Sydney S. Baron and his public relations firm, as I have noted earlier (chapter 7). Baron did not do very much, and the arrangement lasted only a few days. I do not know any more about the termination of this connection than about its beginning.

THE MEDIA: LOCAL AND NATIONAL

After the "bust" on April 29–30, the trustees, at the initiative of the chairman, William E. Petersen, retained the services of Hill and Knowlton, the well-known public relations firm. One of their staff was on the campus, in Low Library, throughout the rest of the spring. His task was a little like reassembling building stones after an earthquake, but he did some very useful things, such as the preparation of the president's "Message to Alumni, Parents and Other Friends of Columbia," which was issued in June. The idea of getting out such an official white paper was not the president's, and he made relatively little use of the Hill and Knowlton representative on his own initiative. That young man, whose name was Eamon Brennan, I saw with some frequency, and I found him bright and skillful as well as congenial. But one man, however talented, could not in a few weeks make up for years of neglect.

In the 1968 crisis, Columbia reaped the results of a bad press over many prior years. Some of this mistreatment was deserved, as a result of faulty policies or of clumsy fumbling of the public relations aspects of defensible policies. One need only recall the Strickman filter fiasco in the summer of 1967 to understand that Columbia might be seen as an institution that was mismanaged and capable of actions that were ethically questionable. In a broader category, Columbia, like many similar institutions in urban areas, in the years after World War II was growing in size and in the complexity of the undertakings in which it was engaged. The gymnasium aside, such growth required expanded facilities. Especially since open land on or near the campus was essentially nonexistent, such expansion necessarily brought the University into conflict with its neighbors. This was inescapable for Columbia, as it was for growing urban institutions in other cities and on Morningside Heights itself. With careful development of plans and particularly with skillful handling of their public relations aspects, such conflict could not be avoided perhaps, but it could be and by some institutions it was minimized. In Columbia's case, as I suggested in chapter 2, neither of these protective conditions existed. The controversy over the "gymnasium in the park" merely aggravated a situation that was already negative.

All this acknowledged, some of the bad press, especially in the *New York Times*, was not fully deserved and could justifiably be attributed to bias or incompetence in the reporting. This was especially conspicuous in the coverage of incidents involving "the community." From time to time, even before the gymnasium project provided a focus, groups of 20 to 50 or so people assembled on or near the campus to demonstrate against something that the University allegedly had done or was planning to do. A favorite site was the northwest corner of 116th Street and Morningside Drive, the location of the President's House. For example, as the Cox Commission reports (pp. 81ff), on July 27, 1967, such a demonstration occurred on this spot, though Cox does not mention that it was the President's House; this one was directed at the gymnasium.

Invariably the press accounts of these events spoke of a protest by "the community." They never noted, however, that in each demonstration "the community" was the same group of 20 of so, augmented from time to time by a few others. Nor did they notice that invariably a conspicuous leader of "the community" group was a woman Marie Runyon whose activities I described in chapter 2. Various efforts were made to correct the inaccuracies and omissions in the reporting on "the community," but without result. The president may even have spoken to Arthur Sulzberger, publisher of the *New York Times*, who was a trustee, but I doubt if that was ever done. In any event, the misrepresentations continued. An enterprising reporter could easily have identified them.

During the crisis itself, the newspaper coverage, though it was somewhat uneven in quality, was quite complete and reasonably objective (in contrast with the television treatment, about which I shall have more to say shortly). Perhaps because neither the rhetoric nor the behavior of the demonstrators was particularly appealing, the *New York Times* supplemented its news reports on more than one occasion with editorials that generally supported the University authorities. For example, see the editorials on April 25 and April 29, 1968. On the former date, the lead editorial, entitled "Hoodlumism at Columbia," said, "The destructive minority of students at Columbia University, along with their not so friendly allies among community militants, have offered a degrading spectacle of hoodlum tactics—the exaltation of irresponsibility over reason." And on the later date the opening sentence of an editorial entitled "Citadel of Reason," read, "The faculty, trustees, and administration of Columbia University have closed ranks against capitulation to the rule-or-ruin tactics of a reckless minority of students."

A few reporters seem to have been persuaded that the demonstrators were idealistic reformers and were not offended by the vulgarity and the widely revolutionary rhetoric of the students. (See *Columbia College Today*, Spring, 1968, p. 62) Other criticisms of the press came from both participants (*Ibid.* p. 91ff) and observers such as Diana Trilling (*Commentary*, November, 1968, p. 43). But a reading of the *New York Times*, which my wife faithfully clipped anything then that would unnecessarily aggravate the situation on the campus.

Despite the inadequacies of the media, Columbia's problems with the news channels were mostly of its own making. They reflected deficiencies of policy, of staffing, of organization, and of leadership that were of long standing. The University was not well equipped to handle the media in calm times. It was hopelessly incapacitated for making its case in a crisis.

CHAPTER TWELVE
WHY 1968?

The question "Why 1968?" must be asked despite the improbability of arriving at a definitive answer. It must be asked because raising the question, whether or not a convincing answer is arrived at, is essential to putting the Columbia crisis in context. Without that the Columbia crisis cannot be understood.

The most important element in the context, as I have suggested in the prologue to this memoir, is the recognition that the 1968 incidents and the campus-based events of the next year or two were part of a phenomenon that was nationwide, almost worldwide. As the late Richard Hofstadter said in his Columbia Commencement Address of June 4, 1968, what had occurred at Columbia "must not be regarded as an isolated incident, since it is only the most severe, among American universities, of a number of such incidents." Without attempting to account for their wider extent, he went on to say, "Not only in New York and Berkeley, but in Madrid and Paris, in Belgrade and Oxford, in Rome, Berlin and London, and on many college and university campuses throughout this country, students are disaffected, restive, and rebellious."

To those who remember this period and to some of those who have read about it, depending on what they have read, Hofstadter's statement should come as no surprise. Events on American campuses were covered in the press, though none as extensively as Columbia's, with the exception of the bloody tragedies at Kent State and Jackson State in 1970. O'Neill reports that "Between January 1 and June 15, 1968, the National Student Association counted 221 major demonstrations at 101 colleges and universities involving nearly forty thousand students. But Columbia, by far the most spectacular, may stand for all the rest." (O'Neill, p. 289)

Newspapers of the day reported many of the events outside of the United States, notably the uprisings in Paris in early May 1968, which resulted, among other startling consequences, in the unprecedented closing of the Sorbonne and the elevation of Daniel Cohn-Bendit (as Danny the Red) to the status of an international celebrity. (See, for example, the *New York Times*, May 4, 1968.) These events in Paris and Nanterre would have surprised no one who had visited the French universities, especially those in Paris, at any time in the previous 20 years and had witnessed the appalling crowding—a fraction of the seats necessary in the libraries, insufficient places in lecture halls, even for standees, and an atmosphere of total indifference to the needs of students.

Commentators have noted in subsequent years the extent of the troubles in the late 1960s. Douglas Knight, writing in 1989, reported that in the spring of 1968 the Association of American Universities (the organization of all the important research universities in the country) had asked him, as president of Duke, and Howard Johnson, president of the Massachusetts Institute of Technology, to call on the Secretary of State and to "represent . . . our collective view of the desperate campus situation." (Knight, *Street of Dreams*, p. 64) He also noted elsewhere (*Ibid*. p. 124), "Our students shared their moral agitation with movements as far removed as France and the Soviet Union. . . . Like canaries in a mine, students were telling us that there was trouble and that it was rapidly getting out of control."

Clearly aware of the extent of the unrest, he did not, for some reason, suggest that the "trouble" might have some common content, which all the "canaries" were signaling. I think that it did, but that is getting ahead of my story.

Others over the years have been more disposed to recognize the near universality of the upheavals of those years. Thus, Richard H. Adrian, master of Pembroke College, Cambridge, in his Henry LaBarre Jayne Lecture to the American Philosophical Society 20 years after the 1968 climax, observed "the universities of North America and Europe and Britain were convulsed by the unrest of 1968–1974. The causes were multiple, some international and some local, but by any standard it was a tragedy which soured a generation of students and left universities defensive and shaken." Similarly, Flora Lewis, writing in 1985 of the combination of local and international factors in these critical events, observed that "Some kind of lightning bolt leapt around the world, igniting tinder that had been accumulating." (*New York Times*, December 27, 1985)

Gradually commentators began to see that the origins of the upheavals were not purely local. As a reviewer noted on an otherwise undistinguished book in 1988, "The best thing about [it] . . . is that it forces us to abandon the easy parochialism with which Americans unthinkingly remember the traumatic spring and summer of 1968." (*New York Times Book Review*, April 3, 1988, p. 8)

Not everyone was so forced, however. In fact, one could and can observe a puzzling tendency for comment on any instance of campus turmoil in these years to assume, at least implicitly, that the situation under discussion was unique, separable, and thus entirely avoidable and, if the will and skill were present, controllable.

Almost certainly the source of this puzzling, even contradictory behavior lies in the situations being inherently political in the generic sense of the word, which implies that the reactions are going to be political. In a "democratic" setting, that means that multiple causes, which are confusing and uncomfortable, providing no immediate and satisfying resolution, must be rejected or ignored. Instead it is necessary to the comfort of the "people" that some one person be held responsible, a person who can without trial be convicted of doing something or failing to do something, which resulted in the disruptive uprising. Scapegoats, localized explanations, are a necessary device for adjustment to a political catastrophe, especially in a "democracy." Typically, therefore, in a disruptive student uprising, the president is disposed of, sometimes immediately and sometimes, as at Harvard following the 1969 disruption there, after a "decent" interval. It is a sort of ritual sacrifice that almost invariably must occur, even if the president's contribution to the crisis has been marginal, as a surfer who is swamped by the bad fortune of riding on the wrong spot on a breaking wave.

Once the culprit has been identified and disposed of, the past is adequately "explained." For the victim, of course, the experience can be devastating, as Douglas Knight indicates with dignity and remarkable restraint: "Those of us in the senior universities felt we stood high in our profession; then one day we found that…we were powerless. Nothing would come right, and we lost our innocence in a singularly painful way even as we lost our careers." (Knight, *Street of Dreams*, p. 81)

The apparent need for even quite sophisticated observers to insist unyieldingly on local, parochial causes is exemplified by Archibald Cox in his report on the Columbia crisis. He speaks in his opening, almost prefatory pages of disturbances similar to those at Columbia taking place in both eastern and western Europe. "These facts alone are enough to suggest that conditions common to many universities were among the underlying causes of the explosion at Columbia." Two sentences later, however, he reverts to the simplicity of localism when he says, "Yet it would be a mistake to conclude that Columbia experienced last spring's disturbances because she was caught in a broader movement beyond her control." (Cox, p. 3)

These lines were written by Cox in the summer of 1968. One cannot help wondering if the equivalent words would have been written of Harvard a year later after the seizure of University Hall, the police action forcibly evicting the occupiers, and the subsequent strike. The Cambridge administration, under Cox's "expert" guidance, made several mistakes, at least some of which could have been avoided if the Columbia experience had been deeply understood. Most notable among these was the failure immediately following the outbreak of the troubles to ask the Faculty of Arts and Sciences to vote for the use of police assistance instead of taking that decision alone and in consequence calling down on the president the full force of the inevitable recriminations. One can have no doubt, however, that, absent the sponsoring international context beyond Harvard's control, the occasion for these mistakes would not have existed,

Nathan Pusey would have served out a full term as Harvard's president, and Franklin Ford would have continued as dean of the Faculty of Arts and Sciences. I am not an apologist for Grayson Kirk, as earlier chapters have made clear, but I cannot deny that, like Pusey and many others, he was a victim as well as, and perhaps as much as, an actor.

Even when the importance of the national-international component in the context is admitted, however, a definitive answer to the key question "Why 1968?" remains elusive. So widespread a phenomenon must have complex and even quite subtle origins.

In some quarters it has been suggested that the Columbia assault was the lead incident in a leftist conspiracy to undermine the society by destroying its major universities. The rhetoric of the SDS frequently had this thrust, and certainly some members of the group were convinced revolutionaries. But anyone close to the organization realized that it lacked the discipline of a genuine conspiracy. Not only were the SDS leaders at Columbia and elsewhere complete opportunists, but their movements generally displayed in fully developed form the chaos that the leaders hoped to induce in the society at large. The conspiracy "explanation" is essentially another escape into simplicity, and it has the further handicap that it does not adequately account for the near-global character of the phenomenon.

If conspiracy did not spawn the movements, how about the contagion of imitation? In a small way, this probably had some influence, certainly within the United States, but probably, with the aid of television, over a wider area. The extensive coverage of the classic use of paving blocks in the Paris barricades on the Left Bank early in May undoubtedly suggested to some of the Columbia activists the tactical utility of the bricks with which the campus walks were paved. But the evidence of imitation is superficial and minor.

We have also been treated to a host of free-wheeling psychological analyses, usually with a limited empirical base, purporting to explain a generation and a decade. These may have been profitable, at least for their authors, and they may have been comforting to those yearning for an explanation. Where these speculations were not irrelevant, they certainly were inconclusive, if only because they were culture-bound. As one commentator has observed, "One can't explain the rebelliousness of university students in Madrid and Mexico City by reference to Benjamin Spock's childrearing advice, or cite students' affluence to understand the aspirations of those who took to the streets in Warsaw, Prague and Paris." (Nelson Lichtenstein in the *New York Times Book Review*, April 3, 1988, p. 8)

Clearly 1968 reflected a complex of general factors, filtered through the particular local conditions that exposed individual institutions in varying degrees to damaging disruption. Some of the latter, as in the Columbia case, were not trivial. And certainly the appalling overcrowding at the Sorbonne amply warranted student resentment. But it was the general factors that were determining and locally uncontrollable.

One fundamental undoubtedly is the range and rapidity of the transformations that the world had experienced in the second half of the twentieth century. Most people, perhaps because they have to, may take for granted the technological revolutions in communication, in transportation, the sharp alterations in political arrangements that

ning of taboos, the voluntary movement
.tions, and the apparent shrinking of the
, of changes are hard to digest, because they
en painful adjustment of learned expectations,
its of thinking.

universities, and ignored by most commentators is what Franc.. Akley had called the single most important set of factors shaping the undergraduate experience of today, namely, the demographic changes of the past thirty years. He identifies especially the "unprecedented increases in the numbers of students crowding into colleges and universities all over the world," a change that has "no historical parallel." Equally unparalleled historically is the diversity of this student population—in religion, social class, age, gender, race, and ethnicity. (Francis Oakley, "Against Nostalgia: Reflections on Our Present Discontents in Higher Education.," National Humanities Center, *Newsletter*, Vol. 12, No. 2, Spring–Summer, 1991.)

Oakley's insights are unassailable. They shrewdly identify "common conditions" and "general factors." The indigestibility of the types of changes that Oakley rightly calls "shaping factors" was evident in the experiences of American students (and others) in the civil rights protests of the early 1960s, was reflected in the so-called Free Speech movement at Berkeley in 1964, and was accentuated by an atmosphere of violence epitomized by the assassination of President Kennedy in 1963, a shocking tragedy that became for many of the rebels of five years later their first political memory.

But the real lightning bolt was supplied by the escalation of the Vietnam War beginning in 1965. As a young reporter for the *New*

York Times named Steven Roberts wrote in May 1968, "The New Left had taken on a new tone of bitterness in the last few years as students who once battled mainly for the rights of Negroes and Vietnamese peasants found themselves facing the draft." (*New York Times*, May 3, 1968)

I am convinced that Vietnam, aided by extensive television coverage, which for the first time brought the horrors of war into the living room, was the lightning bolt that Flora Lewis suspected of igniting world-wide conflagration. And it is important to realize that the impact of the brutality of the Vietnam conflict was indeed worldwide.

Of this extensive impact I had some direct testimony from the comments of a number of European university officials who visited the United States and Columbia University soon after the 1968 outbreak. These included rectors of at least two Scandinavian universities and three or more of their counterparts in West Germany. Each of these officials spoke about local irritations and questioned me about the equivalent factors at Columbia, but all of them emphasized the shock and disillusionment among their students and faculty created by the reporting of Vietnam.

But in a basic sense none of these statements nor any of those that I read in the journals astonished me. I had had the rare good fortune for several weeks in the summer of 1954 and again in the summer and fall of 1962 to spend considerable time visiting in European universities in Sweden, Norway, Denmark, West Germany, France, Italy, and the United Kingdom. I talked with professors, primarily in the humanities and the social sciences, and with many students, particularly graduate students. One of my strongest impressions from that the students were not entitled to an injunction, he "had not meant to hold that they were wrong . . . in all possible respects." He went on to say, "I wonder . . . how many of us have failed to wonder at least once how it must be for those youngsters who think this not only a senseless war, but an evil one. Forget for a minute whether they're right or wrong. Concede only that they could think this way without being utterly vicious. And that many of them do. And then picture how the long nights of decision might feel as the moment approached for the giving or refusal of consent." (Quoted in Lusky and Lusky, pp. 184–185) To this hard dilemma Judge Frankel could have added the cumulative feeling of guilt that they had escaped the draft this long only because they had the good fortune to be in college.

The essence of the answer to "Why 1968?" lies, therefore, in the Vietnam war and what it did, not just to American universities and their students, but to America's standing in the eyes of students over most of the globe, students who, along with many of their mentors, had idealized the United States. In their disillusionment they turned in a kind of desperation against the local objects of their often wholly legitimate resentment.

EPILOGUE

Behind this Columbia story another can be told, although I probably shall not write it. That story is implicit in much that I have written in these pages. It has to do with friendships, colleagueships, that I treasure. It has to do with the pride that I felt in joining the Columbia faculty and in being one of a group of scholars of standing and substance with whom it was an inspiration to be associated. It has to do, as I suggested in the opening pages of this story, with why I felt deep pain and irreparable loss when I decided that I should sever my connections with Columbia after 19 years. It is a better story.

REMARKS
AT COLUMBIA UNIVERSITY
October 23, 2003

On October 23, 2003, at the initiative of President Lee Bollinger and Provost Alan Brinkley, Columbia University hosted a Celebration of the Life of David Bicknell Truman in St. Paul's Chapel on the Morningside Heights Campus. University Chaplain Jewelnel Davis arranged the service, which was followed by a reception in the Trustees Room of Low Memorial Library.

The words that were spoken in St. Paul's Chapel went some way toward fleshing out the Epilogue to my father's memoir. Therefore, we reproduce here, with permission, the principal remarks on that occasion in the order in which they spoke: Alan Brinkley, provost of Columbia University; Judge José Cabranes of the United States Court of Appeals for the Second Circuit and trustee of Columbia University; Fritz Stern, historian and Columbia University Professor Emeritus; Warner R. Schilling, James T. Shotwell Professor of International Relations Emeritus; and Peter Pouncey, former dean of Columbia College and president emeritus of Amherst College. (President Bollinger spoke first, but we do not have a copy of his remarks. My own remarks are largely captured in the brief biography of my father that follows.)

Provost Alan Brinkley

I first became aware of my distinguished predecessor, David Truman, when—as a freshman at Princeton taking my first political science course—I read his book *The Governmental Process* [New York, Knopf, 1951, second edition. 1971], a great, pioneering classic that advanced the phrase, and much of the modern idea of "interest groups" in scholarly discourse and, in the process, posed a powerful challenge to classical liberal theory. Prior to Truman, most scholars, and most political commentators, considered interest groups to be unhealthy organisms in the body politic that undermined democracy. But Truman argued that we should not worry so much about interest groups—that they in fact help advance democracy by representing coherent interests rather than individual passions, and that in any case most individuals have varied and cross-cutting interests which prevent any one interest group from becoming central. For nearly a generation, this idea—which became known as "group theory"—dominated a large area of academic inquiry.

The book is still in print and still widely read today; I stumbled on a recent review from one of its readers, a political science student in California, on Amazon.com just this week, which said:

> This is probably the best reference book for any political science student interested in Group Theory. I would also recommend work by V. O. Key and Robert Dahl, but Truman's work has been the most useful to me. . . . I have about 23 books at my feet right now as I work on a paper for my Masters Degree, but I find myself picking up *Governmental Process* more than any other.

REMARKS AT COLUMBIA UNIVERSITY

I read *The Governmental Process* in the spring of 1968, a season of great turbulence in America and at Columbia, a time when the liberal democratic world that David Truman so brilliantly analyzed and in which he so deeply believed seemed to many people to be falling apart. He left the university the following year to become a distinguished president of Mount Holyoke College and, later, the president of the Russell Sage Foundation. But we are here today to remember above all his life at this university, of which he was such an important part for nearly two decades—a great scholar and teacher, a dynamic department chair, a popular and energetic dean of the College, and a courageous provost in a time of crisis.

In 1979, shortly after he left Mount Holyoke, he gave an interview about his career to the political scientist Donald Stokes, in which, among other things, he described his arrival on this campus in 1950, coming with no previous experience of the University. I find in his perceptive and loving comments about Columbia an echo of my own experience as a newcomer to the University (four decades after Truman's arrival), having spent years studying and teaching elsewhere.

> I was the man who came to dinner, because I went there in the fall of 1950 for a one-year visit and stayed for nineteen years. I loved Columbia [almost at once] . . . There's a pulse about the place, the pulse of New York . . . I loved the undergraduate teaching in the College at Columbia as I have not [loved] any other that I've ever done . . . That was the most exciting group of undergraduates I've ever had. . . . [There was] a kind of democracy of the intellect about Columbia. . . . You knew you were being listened to if you had something to say, and if you didn't have anything to say it didn't matter what your rank was, you were going to be ignored. And at the

same time [there was] a kind of generosity of spirit and intellect that I never encountered in quite the same way anywhere else.

He had an almost intuitive understanding of the special qualities of this remarkable university, an understanding that helped him rise rapidly through its ranks. He was a great champion of the College; a great defender of the integrity of the academic life; and most of all both a profound critic and passionate defender of liberal democracy – a contested and (in his time at Columbia) sometimes maligned concept that he never ceased to believe had a rich and robust meaning. I never met David Truman, but I will remember him—with admiration and with tremendous gratitude for his contributions to the life of ideas and to this great institution.

Judge José A. Cabranes

Members of the Truman family and friends and admirers of David Truman:

I come before you not as an intimate or as a professional colleague of David B. Truman, but simply as a student in the Truman era at Columbia College (class of 1961)—and one who shares with his contemporaries an abiding respect for David Truman as a scholar, teacher, and academic leader.

I am now a trustee of the great University David Truman served with distinction, honor, and sacrifice. And so I feel doubly honored, as an alumnus *and* as a trustee, to be able to join in this celebration of his long and productive life.

David Truman was a special favorite of the College. We are reminded by the recently-published history of Columbia that his tenure as professor of government and dean of the College was so successful that in 1967 he was offered the provostship of Stanford, triggering a successful campaign by the College's faculty, students, and alumni for his appointment as provost of Columbia, where he became, in the words of our historian, the "odds-on choice [of the trustees] to be [the] successor" to a president not far from retirement. (Robert A. McCaughey, *Stand Columbia: A History of Columbia University in the City of New York, 1754–2004*, New York, Columbia University Press, 2003, p. 419)

Even before he was dean, Professor Truman was a vivid presence around Hamilton Hall and the Van Am Quadrangle. The obituary in the *New York Times* (September 1, 2003) had it right when it described him as follows:

> Short, stocky and heavy-browed, with a beret to shield him from the stiff winds on Morningside Heights, he seemed to embody the vigor and optimism of the Kennedy and early Johnson years.
>
> He presided over the liberalizing of ancient, unpopular rules, allowing Columbia [College] men to close their doors when they had women in their rooms and instituting a two-day break between the end of classes and final exams. He spoke out for civil rights and against McCarthyism, and publicly challenged [one colleague's] famous assertion that the liberal arts were "dead or dying." As dean, he liked to drop in and chat with students in their dorm rooms. At a college assembly in 1966, the students gave him a standing ovation.

He had been recommended for the position of dean of the College in 1963 by a faculty search committee headed by no less a figure than Professor Lionel Trilling, the reigning intellectual figure at Columbia in the post-war period. Our historian reports that Truman had "a considerable reputation as a scholar," unlike many of his predecessors, and thus some of his colleagues were surprised "when he enthusiastically agreed to take the administrative job [dean of Columbia College]." (McCaughey, p. 419)

The reasons for this surprise are embedded in Columbia's history. The College faculty, we are reminded, "regarded the teaching of undergraduates as a noble calling," and its faculty resented its "subordination . . . by their graduate school colleagues, by the faculty of the professional schools, and by the administrators in Low Library." (*Ibid.* p. 422)

One cause of the alienation of the College faculty was the fact that, since the mid-nineteenth century, virtually every Columbia president had been a so-called "[Columbia] College Skeptic," preoccupied not with undergraduate education, but instead, with management of the ever-burgeoning academic sprawl they conceived to be a true house of intellect. (*Ibid.* p. 422)

Truman was no "College Skeptic." And we all knew it.

When he was appointed provost of the University in 1967 he "surprised" Columbia again. The surprise this time was that into the inner sanctum of Low Library had moved, "a [Columbia] College Believer if there ever was one"—let us savor that phrase: *not* a "[Columbia] College Skeptic," *but rather*, "a [Columbia] College Believer if there ever was one." (*Ibid.* p. 422)

A graduate of Amherst and a former member of the faculty of Williams, Truman had unabashed fondness for the small college in a huge university—the small college with the famously demanding core curriculum; the small college heavily populated by intellectually curious and aggressive students from newly-arrived ethnic communities of New York City, many of whom, in that era, would have been brushed off by places like Yale and Princeton as a result of long-accepted, but nevertheless invidious, discrimination; the small college [was] substantially responsible for the reputation of the larger university.

I first encountered David Truman in the textbook of the basic course in United States Government taught by Professor Julian H. Franklin ("Government 5–6," if memory serves). The book was *The Governmental Process: Political Interests and Public Opinion.*

This remarkable book—first published in 1951 and lovingly dedicated to Ellie and Ted, the author wrote, as "a token of gratitude as well as a mark of affection"—was one of the earliest, and most important, systematic studies of the role of interest groups in the American political process.

The book did not ignore what Professor Truman called "[t]he formalities of legal structure," which had preoccupied earlier writers, but its very title—*The Governmental Process*—marked the book as part of the emerging political behavior movement in political science, which looked upon politics as a series of dynamic, often informal, interactions among key participants.

Reconsidering the book a half a century after its initial publication, I am struck by the values that animated David Truman's work so long ago and that would mark his own work in the process of governing institutions of higher education: "a preference for the essential features of representative democracy, and . . . a belief in the virtues of peaceful change;" the importance of a common understanding of the "rules of the game" that, in his words, "clearly include the acceptance of the rule of law over a resort to violence or to arbitrary official action, the guarantees of the Bill of Rights, effective modes of mass participation . . . and a measure of equality of access to the fruits of the social enterprise." (Truman, *The Governmental Process*, p. xi and p. xxxvii)

More than half a century after its publication, I am struck also by the deep sympathy of the author, well before the flowering of the modern civil rights movement for the "interest groups" devoted to ending the American system of apartheid.

Apart from brief contacts on the campus, my next serious encounter with Professor Truman was at his home. The Truman home on Morningside Heights was the only home of a Columbia professor which I ever entered as an undergraduate—and, for reasons that defy explanation today, I was not even one of the fortunate students to have Professor Truman as a classroom teacher.

I do not recall why or how I came to be favored by an invitation to a buffet dinner at the Truman home, to meet the celebrated critic and sometime Trotskyite Dwight Macdonald. But it was, for me, a memorable evening.

When I came to know Professor Truman better, a generation later, as a fellow trustee of The Twentieth Century Fund, I enjoyed telling him that, in the innocence of my youth in the outer boroughs of New York City, I had never before *met* a real, honest-to-goodness Trotskyite.

In the years of the Truman deanship in the mid-1960s, I was privileged to be awarded a Kellett Fellowship to study international law at Cambridge University, and in the mid-1960s Truman—always a celebrator of the College and its students—did something that at the time was quite remarkable: He held a fine candle-lit dinner on campus for the sole purpose of bringing together, and recognizing, generations of Kellett Fellows.

Today this sort of gesture, like the invitation to dinner at his home, may not seem particularly remarkable to you. At the time, it was. For me the dinner for the Kellett Fellows was but another sign that Truman was "a [Columbia] College Believer if ever there was one," and so much the better for all concerned.

Not only in print, but in life and in his whole career at Columbia, and later at Mount Holyoke College, David Truman was liberal, decent, open, and generous, and he always understood the virtues of compromise except on matters of basic principle.

In reading David Truman's "Reflections on the Columbia Disorders of 1968," written a quarter of a century after that trauma, one is struck by Truman's ability, with dispassion and nuance, to distinguish between two principal groups of student activists— "the white extremists [who] had passed their childhood years in the 'better' sections of the city or the comfortable suburbs" and "most of the blacks [, who] came from families who have lived near or below the poverty line in the central cities [,] who did not have it made, [and who] knew it, which marked their actions with a kind of courage and integrity that was a good deal less evident [among the white extremists]." (David B. Truman, "Reflections on the Columbia Disorders of 1968," Columbia University Archives, 1992; revised 1995, p. 72)

He describes the group of black students who occupied Hamilton Hall and ejected the white extremists as "in general . . . highly unified and remarkably disciplined[,]" noting "the fact of their dignified and disciplined conduct throughout the whole affair." (*Ibid*, pp. 81-82)

This respect was mutual. In February 1969, when he was about to leave the University to lead another great American college, Dave Truman was asked to attend a dinner that the black students of the College were having at the Faculty Club. Typically, Truman agreed. It was only after he arrived at the Faculty Club that he learned that the dinner was in his honor. "I had a number of compliments paid to me as I left Columbia," he wrote, "but none was greater and none moved me more than that one." (*Ibid*, p. 83)

That is the gracious, measured, and honorable man the Columbia College students of the 1950s and 1960s knew and the man they will remember always—with affection, admiration, respect, and gratitude.

Professor Fritz Stern

The 1950s and early 1960s were a time of astounding intellectual vibrancy at Columbia. I doubt that any other institution could have matched the unpretentious seriousness of Columbia, the innovativeness of so many of its faculty. At the time we were more aware of our shortcomings than our blessings, but the latter made life exciting and worthwhile for teachers and students. David Truman was one of the luminaries of that time; he embodied that quiet greatness, that devotion to scholarship and collegial humanity that made Columbia special. As a teacher and a dean he was respected and cherished: we admired his formidable intellect, his wisdom, his dedication, and we took courage and inspiration from the man. Above all, he had our trust, for we knew he was a man of unshakable integrity. I hope he felt the often-unexpressed affection we had for him.

I wish we could have said to him that he was a model scholar–citizen, but our culture inhibits such avowals. Others are better qualified to speak about his scholarship; I am in awe of the force of his work, composed while fulfilling so many other commitments. Consider a new dean of the College writing a landmark presidential speech to the American Political Science Association: the sheer energy that brought brilliance to paper. He was a master analyst of American politics and government; scholarship and civic commitment reinforced each other. In our own anguished times, it is appropriate to recall that he was a true patriot, cognizant of our exceptional place among nations, aware of the collapse of other democracies, and concerned that thoughtless, selfish citizens might forget the potential fragility of our own democracy. His text for students warned that "no guarantee can be found against the possibility that events will produce a shift [of our government] toward an authoritarian form." American politics have changed since his masterly studies, but his deep, informed concern about the future of the polity, about the health and justice of our society, is timelier than ever. He was a political scientist in the best tradition: rigorous in empirical detail, aware of historical circumstance and contingency, and infused by a deep moral sense—to say nothing of his passion for clarity; his scorn for sloppiness. He was a liberal who practiced conservative virtues, among them, realism and lucidity.

I was privileged to know him especially well in the 1960s, as the College dean. He entrusted me with various tasks, and one didn't say "no" to Dave. And he didn't say no to me when I assembled a group of historians and political scientists in 1965 to see what, if anything, we might do to help extricate this country from a disastrous and divisive war in Vietnam. We shared other and related concerns: in the same year, we both addressed the College on student unrest, a phenomenon that had left most administrators and faculty undisturbed. Dave acknowledged "there are plenty of reasons around us today for anyone to be restless and to be worried. . . . One cannot ignore the very widespread uncertainty, self-pity, timidity, and, yes, even hypocrisy that exists today in the adult environment." He sensed some of the deeper causes of unrest, the feeling "there must be something more to life than a house in the suburbs, the two-car family, and television." But he warned against nihilistic temptations, against forgetting that the students' "larger purposes can be achieved only through institutions—institutions which they may criticize and which they may attempt to alter, but which ultimately they must protect if civilized life is to continue. . . . Protest and criticism are essential to the life of this society," but ends could never be independent of means.

We encountered student protest in inflammatory concentration in 1968, in the year of our collective misery: the year of assassinations in the United States and of the Soviet extinction of the Prague spring. Much has been written about Columbia in 1968 and about the year 1968 generally: the causes of the protest were many and mixed, the responses of a divided faculty and administration often ill-considered, but despite all the faddish mythologizing, I think 1968 at Columbia was a violent assault on one of the freest and most fragile institutions of the country, the liberal university.

It is to the credit of Columbia and to the traditions that Dave Truman exemplified that this university recovered in time, battered and sobered. It is not my purpose here to relive those painful days when raw emotion and unreason swept over us, but I doubt that anyone in the Provost's position of that time could have better defended our principles of freedom and non-violence than did Dave Truman.

Let me end with some personal reminiscences. I still have Dave's letter from Rome, Christmas Eve 1962—before he had even assumed the deanship—telling me his plans for the College and encouraging me to stay at Columbia. Nor can I forget the night in Low Library in 1968, at some grim moment, perhaps the second bust, when bricks were smashing through the window of his office, and we were crouching beneath his desk. I had complained about a fatuous harangue of one of his colleagues at a critical meeting, and Dave said in infinite admonitory gentleness: "Oh, Fritz, he just bores you."

What Columbia lost in 1969, Mount Holyoke gained, when Dave became its president. And my daughter, a student there a year later, cherished an inspiring president; she wrote me for this occasion: "I have always wanted to thank Dave and Ellie for the way they welcomed me to MHC—always encouraging and always willing to talk as family friends, as president of the College, and as husband and wife. Never mincing words, they told me how life was . . ."

To Ellie and Ted and Tracy, our thanks for the joy and support they brought into Dave's life. He cherished his home and family, at heart he was a private man. And for myself, the deepest gratitude for his friendship. And as an old Columbian, the expression of our collective and affectionate gratitude for a great and memorable colleague.

Professor Warner Schilling

I want to talk a bit about Dave Truman's contribution as a political scientist and also as a colleague in what was then called the Department of Public Law and Government. I should note that Dick Neustadt has written, in his usual clear and moving prose, a more detailed account of Dave's contributions to political science as a scholar that will appear in *PS—Political Science & Politics*, a publication of the American Political Science Association and that I have borrowed a few points from Dick's account.

Dave received his Ph.D. in 1939 from the University of Chicago. In those years, the Chicago political science department was unique in encouraging its students to look widely at psychology, economics, and sociology for the information and approaches that might be useful in their own work, and they even had a course on quantitative analysis in political science. It was this training, coupled with his undergraduate major in history, that was responsible for the fact that Dave always took a very catholic approach to what constituted productive work in political science.

After graduation, Dave taught first at Bennington and then at Cornell, but when we entered the war, he went promptly to Washington, serving first as a civilian in various government offices and then as a naval officer for the Joint Chiefs of Staff. Following the war, he taught at Harvard, which he found too traditional in its approach to political science, and then at Williams. It was from there that Columbia lured him as a visiting associate professor in 1950, and, happily for us, as a full professor in 1951.

This was also the year in which he published a truly outstanding book, *The Governmental Process*. This had already gone through 11 printings by 1965 and was republished [as a second edition with a new introduction] in 1971 and again in 1981. As Dick Neustadt notes in *PS—Political Science & Politics*, "The sophistication of [his] concepts . . . makes the book still more relevant, after more than 50 years." A second book, *The Congressional Party*, was published in 1959, reflecting the years that Dave had labored so long and hard in the Social Science Research Council trying to foster the development of work on Congress and public opinion.

The academic honors that followed these and other publications were many. He was, for example, a Guggenheim fellow, a fellow of the American Academy of Arts and Sciences, and a member of the American Philosophical Society. In 1967, he was a vice president of the American Association for the Advancement of Science and, as you know, in 1964–65, the president of the American Political Science Association.

Dave was a popular and effective teacher of both undergraduate and graduate students, but Columbia undergraduates were clearly his favorites. In an interview in 1979 [with Donald Stokes], he said, "I loved the undergraduate teaching in the College at Columbia as I have not any other that I've ever done." He also could be, when needed, a demanding teacher. Dick Neustadt quotes one graduate student who produced a first-rate dissertation as explaining, "He forced it out of me. He wouldn't take less for an answer."

Dave was also a most effective leader and administrator. I heard him once say that the task of leadership was to absorb uncertainty. I can testify that he practiced what he preached. Dave was the departmental representative for the College when I came to Columbia, and he had to absorb an awful lot of uncertainty from me. I was not only a novice teacher, I was a most insecure and anxious one. Dave's style was calm, steady, and leavened with quiet, ironic humor. My course couldn't be too bad, he once assured me, because no one had come to complain to him yet.

But my favorite remark was when I showed him one of my first mid-term examinations. I was very proud of the examination; it was full of long, ingenious provocative quotations, including even one from a novel, and the students were invited to analyze them for a grand total of 50 minutes. Dave read the two full pages of single-spaced quotations and questions on the exam and quietly said, "Those are very interesting questions, Warner. Did the students have any time to answer them?" Well, I learned the lesson!

In those years, those of us teaching in the College met separately as a department. Although I was only a lowly lecturer, teaching one course (my major appointment was as a research associate in the Institute of War and Peace Studies), Dave welcomed me to the department. It was a lively group: Dave, Dick Neustadt, Herb Deane, Julian Franklin, Joe Rothchild, Peter Gay, Ken Waltz, and Guenther Lewy among others. As we met to discuss our curriculum and the state of political science, I found myself developing a sense of profession and professionalism that was as rewarding as it was exciting, and *that* was Dave's leadership.

In due course, I became an assistant professor and began attending the meetings of the full department and found the same spirit there. The department was in those years, as Dick later wrote to me, "the best department that you and I will ever know." It was a department marked by an extraordinary degree of civility and collegiality. Not once in all those years did we ever hold an election or take a vote; a record for which, as political scientists, we were justifiably proud. What made this possible, of course, was not just the talent, but more importantly the character and judgment of the senior members, and among these, Dave, who chaired the department from 1959 until he became dean of the College, was central.

I find it impossible to talk about Dave without saying a word about Elinor. Throughout their marriage, she has been as integral a part of Dave's professional life as she has been to his personal life whether it was helping to devise an indexing system for the Roper Poll Collection at Williams or, when Dave became dean at Columbia, hosting a series of dinners for College faculty at which members of different departments had a chance to meet each other. To that same end, she also presided over faculty teas every Thursday afternoon.

Elinor Truman gave the first dinner party to which my wife and I were invited at Columbia. I found both her and her down-to-earth manner very attractive, and I became a member of the Ellie Truman fan club that very night. Ellie also shares Dave's capacity for absorbing uncertainty. In 1968, I happened to run across Ellie as I emerged from one of the faculty meetings we had been holding after the police had been called on campus. I was in tears of anger and dismay over the recognition that Dave's career at Columbia was at an end. The mark of Ellie's character is that *she* immediately undertook *to console me*!

Nineteen sixty-eight, for those of us who were centrally involved, was a war. We won't talk about it, but it is hard to escape the memories. Suffice it to say that Dave had an extraordinary talent for leadership, but he faced an overwhelming task. He had to cope not only with the SDS and a large number of students, and faculty, who used the university as a surrogate for their own frustrations with the government of the United States. He had also to deal with the interventions of a self-appointed faculty group who, for one reason or another, thought they could do a better job of resolving the issues than the administration.

In addition, Dave had to contend with negotiations, of which few were aware, with various city politicians, the trustees, the New York Police, and his own president. And he did this without once losing control of his emotions in public, which is more than I can say about a lot of us at the time. I speak not, of course, of what he may have vented in private to Ellie.

I have always felt that events would have gone differently if the faculty had been more united in its support, but that alas was not to be. For myself, there are more than a few things in my academic career I now wish I had done differently, but my support for Dave Truman in 1968 is most definitely not one of them. For I thought then and think now that he was dead right on the central issues involved.

It has been my good fortune, then, to know and work with a few people whose outstanding talent was matched by an equally exceptional character. Dave Truman was one. For the opportunity to have been his colleague, I have always considered myself most fortunate indeed.

President Peter Pouncey

David Truman was a political scientist of sharp insight into the structures and behaviors of institutions for good or ill, and he was also deepened by a richly layered sense of history. I will start with an example. On June 10, 1964, as dean of Columbia College, he gave his

REMARKS AT COLUMBIA UNIVERSITY

Class Day address on the theme of "The Gift of Enduring Self," a self without self-pity, to give it Archibald MacLeish's full phrase. This was, David said, the College's 100th Class Day, a centennial pairing it in association with the first, in June of 1865, which immediately presented his young men with a grim parallel with their predecessors—both classes had had their last year in school shadowed by the assassination of the president of the United States, Lincoln and Kennedy. The 1964 class's yearbook was out as he spoke, and had been dedicated by its young editor, Allen Sperling (he named him), to the memory of JFK with an innocent and elegiac inscription: In the hope that our unity of sorrow can produce a unity of purpose. And David then moved on with compassion to speak of the bewilderment and shock of the young generation: could the measured rhythms and cadences of the academy have given any real preparation for the larger and more violent arena into which they were being cast. More particularly, what strength could they count on? David insisted that mind, heart, and spirit are strong or weak depending on the sureness or slackness with which an individual lays hold of tested coherent values, ideas, images, urgencies to straighten him, hold him upright, and drive him on; and he quotes some good gnarled phrases of Robert Frost's prose to nail his point down—"the way the will has to pitch into commitments deeper and deeper to a rounded conclusion, and then be judged whether any original intention it had, has been strongly spent or weakly lost—be it in art, politics, school, church, business, love or marriage—in a piece of work or a career." And then Frost glosses one of his phrases, almost, at first glance, contradicting himself: "strongly spent," he says, "is synonymous with kept." What you spend, you often cannot keep—but you can, of course, if it's faith or commitment. These were the days of standing ovations and faculty memos to trustees urging that commitments be made to David Truman, ensuring his continued presence at Columbia. It was known there were several prestigious places interested in stealing him. It was still four years until all that euphoric esteem would be undone, and his own personal faith tested by the turmoil of 1968, the turmoil of the war and the draft, of new questions of race and community, the turmoil of anger in the streets and in the buildings, when such phrases as "the measured rhythms and cadences of the academy" and even "unity of purpose" came to have a far-away, wistful ring, as of lost innocence.

David Truman was a political scientist in a department, it always seemed to me, of a surprising numbers of grown-ups, and like his colleagues, he could apply his skills astutely to local conditions; their culture spread over the campus, and even we young instructors knew his friend Wallace Sayre's First Law: that in the academy the politics are always the meanest and most bitterly fought because the stakes are so low. The full text of the law actually contains various articles, codicils, and amendments, one of which should be mentioned: academics tend to hurt themselves by an intellectual disdain for the obvious. "Subtle" is a hurray word in the academy, but "obvious" is a boo word: nothing is quite as it seems, there must be a subtext, a barely audible leitmotiv riding under the theme, a hidden motive below the declared fact. To move this to neutral ground, in Austria in 1838, when Metternich was brought news that his great rival Talleyrand had finally died in France, he is said to have narrowed his eyes, and murmured, "I wonder why he did that."

REMARKS AT COLUMBIA UNIVERSITY

Dave Truman read the politics, but he did not play them. When Thomas Hoving at his desk as Park Commissioner fired off a well publicized denunciation of Columbia for encroaching on public parks (despite a city contract to do so in this case), but then a short time later made his own swift land-grab into Central Park in his new position as Director of the Metropolitan Museum, Dave remarked mildly that it was perhaps just a classic illustration of the political proposition that where you stand often depends on where you sit. In 1968, he was undone by serving under a president frozen into immobility; he was of a temperament to act, but he could not act, and as Thucydides was the first to observe, in wartime opportunity waits for no man. The trajectory of that swiftly-rising career was cut, and seemed to some grounded, but again, his judgment on the president is restrained: "He was a man who preferred to preside than to lead, and so, in sum, he was a man for some seasons."

The reason David Truman did not play the politics of academe was that for him the stakes were too high. He was a man enraptured by the high romantic vision of a university, a place where brilliant gifted people drive themselves for a lifetime to the arduous work of thinking new in their chosen field, sometimes across the currents of other people's thoughts, but always supporting each other in a climate of trust and tolerance. It was the discovery that the delicate fabric of trust and tollerance did not hold, could be in fact torn in these troubles, rather than any mishap to himself, that brought him down to depression—from which he was saved by Ellie's and his family's love, and his own strong spirit.

I did not know David in those early days. My first year teaching at Columbia was that pyrotechnic year 1967–68, and I would see him always from a distance, a compact figure moving resolutely and with dignity to another embattled meeting. I admired him, and after it was over, and the record of his 19 years at the University sadly closed, I came to know him and admire him more, well schooled in Truman lore often through the stories of his many friends, and especially our close mutual friend Herbert Deane. When I was inaugurated at Amherst I asked him to speak for me, an alumnus and trustee of Amherst, (and, in fact, the patriarch of three generations of Amherst alumni, all of them Hall-of-Famers,), the seventh dean of Columbia College, and a Five College president. He had walked ahead of me to places I wanted to go. At the end of his memoir on 1968, there is a graceful, tantalizing paragraph in which he says, "I probably shan't write it, but there is a better story." My David Truman comes from the time of the better story. So I will end by telling you a few moments from it. He was of course exactly the same man, but happy and fulfilled; he was supremely blessed in the woman he married, his son and family, his quality undimmed and undiminished by his ordeal.

At the end of my first year, he returned to Amherst to celebrate his 50th anniversary with his classmates, the Amherst College class of 1935, 100 percent of all living members in attendance. There they sat in the sunlight, in the pink of health, in their well-pressed summer suits, still burnished by their Florida winter tans, while Dave addressed them. He delicately sketched in the climate in which they had come to college in 1931, in the teeth of the depression, the sacrifices they and their families had made; he added to it the sense of Amherst's own decline in this period, a time of public doubt and self-doubt still holding the campus after the removal of its greatest president Alexander Meiklejohn in 1923. He then, ever forthright, proceeded efficiently to remove the last leg of their self esteem: "But you will say," he continued, "we were carefully chosen. Well, yes and no. Mostly no." And of course, it turned out that he had checked the admission figures, and every single applicant from any state other than the northeast had been admitted. I thought I saw a brief spasm of discomfort pass over some of the old boys' faces at this unhappy revelation. But they knew Dave and he knew them, so it was all right. And then he moved on to talk quietly about what they had taken with them from their time together, and what had kept them going when they were all thrown into the maelstrom of World War II, some five years off. It was in essence the same speech and the same insistence as his Class Day speech of 1964. It is what you stand for, and the strength with which you stand for it, that keeps you standing through hard times.

He was in fine, feisty form that weekend, I remember. More than 2,000 people back for their various reunions, the campus more densely populated over these few days than during the regular school year (let's hear it for these small devoted colleges!). He had watched me scurrying at least punctually from group to group, and remarked, "Peter, it has not escaped my notice that you don't goof off quite as much as you claim." The line clearly stands at several carefully calculated removes from an actual compliment, but it has delighted me ever since. At the time, I said something like "I am flattered that you should think so." And he smiled his sweet, seraphic smile and said, "Don't be flattered."

Dave had no patience with the thought that his career was destroyed by 1968. Altered, yes, but destroyed certainly not. There was no vanity in the man, no snobbery of rank or status. If there was useful work to be done and gifted intelligent people to be helped—what could be better? The loss was Columbia's. If he had become Columbia's president, as seemed in the natural order of things, likely, he would, I think, have performed the hitherto impossible feat of pulling together the innumerable, astonishing parts into one high-spirited whole. But he was never one to allow himself to dwell on might-have-beens. The most I ever heard in the way of regret, was once, when we were talking about Columbia, the soft, wondering exclamation "O the talents of that place."

He was the best listener I have known, the brown eyes under the strong forehead giving a new meaning to the words "eye contact," never leaving your face as you tried to thread the lines of a thought together; and when he spoke he was the best at summing up his understanding of any matter—the selection of the most salient facts, the key range of opinion on the facts, and the most refined judgment proceeding from facts and opinion together.

Like all truly large souls and characters, he embraced the opposites; he was strong and gentle to the point of tenderness; he had deep veins of humor embedded in the most serious disposition; he commanded great swathes of information, but was most interested in steering it to the most sensible and humane conclusions. He was, in sum, a man for all seasons.

So it is good that after all these years, we bring him back in our memories to this place where he spent 19 treasured years, and at this juncture give our personal thanks for what he did.

DAVID BICKNELL TRUMAN
June 1, 1913–August 28, 2003

David Bicknell Truman was the son of Jane Mackintosh Truman, who was born in Salt Lake City in 1876 and died in 1959 at the age of 82, and Malcolm George Truman, who was also born in 1876, but in Chicago, and died in 1937 at the age of 61.

Like many in his generation, my father was born at home in Evanston, Illinois. He was the third of four children with two older brothers and one younger sister. His father was in the lumber business. Soon after my father's birth, the family moved to a large house on Sheridan Avenue with a back yard running down to Lake Michigan. Upon graduating from Evanston Township High School, he received the Oliver Baty Cunningham Award given to the senior who, in the opinion of his classmates, best exemplifies the qualities of leadership, public service, and academic achievement.

The next stop was Amherst College, where my father majored in history with a de facto minor in political science and graduated in 1935. He was editor of the *Student* and made some enemies within the college administration and among his fellow students for an editorial denouncing President Stanley King's emphasis on football. He also joined with a group of students that interrupted a meeting of the

Board of Trustees to demand that they authorize the building of better athletic facilities at the College. Subsequently, construction was begun on the Alumni Gymnasium. In his senior year, he was part of a group that returned to the College a statue of Sabrina, Goddess of the Britons, which had become the focus of a dangerous inter-class rivalry. (Their effort to end the Sabrina rivalry was only a temporary success.)

Choosing to pursue a graduate degree in political science rather than to attend law school, my father completed his Ph.D. at the University of Chicago in 1939. Chicago was a vibrant institution at the time, and graduate students came in contact with new methods based on other social sciences such as sociology, psychology, economics, and anthropology. He studied with Charles Merriam, the political reformer; Harold Lasswell the sociologist and political scientist; and Quincy Wright, a pioneer in international relations, and came in contact with the work of Arthur Bentley who is often described as a behavioral scientist whose book, *The Process of Government*, published in 1908, introduced the concept of constructive interest groups into the lexicon of American government if not public perceptions. He later taught from that book, which inspired the title for his own book, *The Governmental Process: Political Interests and Public Opinion*. (New York, Knopf, 1951, second edition, 1971)

A fellow Amherst graduate, John Gaus (class of 1915), one of the founders of the field of public administration who was then a professor at the University of Wisconsin but visited Chicago, provided the idea and financial support for my father's dissertation. His dissertation was published by the University of Chicago Press in

1940: *Administrative Decentralization: A Study of the Chicago Field Offices of the United States Department of Agriculture*. This experience introduced my father to Washington and helped to develop his skills as an interviewer, which involved asking good questions and listening closely to answers.

Toward the end of his graduate studies, with some prospect that he could afford the financial responsibility, my father married Elinor Griffenhagen. She was the daughter of Edwin O. and Christine A. Griffenhagen, who lived in Chicago. Her father was one of the founders of the management consultant profession and, among other distinctions, was responsible for the design of many U.S. state civil service systems in the inter-war period of good government reforms. Ellie was a 1936 graduate of Smith College. My parents first met while they were in college and became good friends. The romance came later.

In 1939 jobs for new holders of Ph.D. degrees in any field were not easy to come by. My parents had a choice between a one-year appointment as an instructor at the very new Bennington College, founded in 1932, and a position at Victoria University in Wellington, New Zealand, that came only with payment for a one-way passage. My father later observed that he chose Bennington because he thought that the odds against "writing his way back" from New Zealand to the United States were long. Bennington was an exciting institution, and my parents made friends among students and faculty that lasted for the rest of their lives. However, the contract ran out after a second year. My parents next moved to Ithaca, New York, and an instructor's position at Cornell for the 1941–42 academic year. That was where they were on December 7, 1941, listening to the

Metropolitan Opera when the program was interrupted with news of the Japanese attack on Pearl Harbor.

My father was one of many immediately drawn into government service, not because he was drafted—his age of 28 and my birth six months previously prevented that—but out a sense of obligation. As his Mount Holyoke College colleague Richard Johnson puts it, "Truman was part of a generation of social scientists who were thrown together in Washington during World War II, continuing their mutual education while helping to fight that war." (Richard A. Johnson, "David Bicknell Truman: 1 June 1913 – 28 August 2003," *Proceedings of the American Philosophical Society*, Vol. 150, No. 4, December 2006, p. 699) He started working part time in Washington in early 1942 while still teaching at Cornell, but he later took leave. He worked, first, at the Office of Price Administration before moving to the analysis staff of the Foreign Broadcast Intelligence Service, which was then part of the Federal Communications Commission, and finally to become deputy head of the Division of Program Surveys in the Department of Agriculture, which conducted opinion surveys for various federal agencies, including the War Bond Division of the U.S. Treasury Department.

Ultimately his sense of duty and civilian status in a city where most of the young men were in uniform led my father in 1944 to volunteer for the Navy. He expected to be sent to the Pacific. Instead, he changed his clothes, his salary was cut in half, and he was assigned to a large steel desk. He ended up as assistant secretary of the Joint Production Survey Committee of the Joint Chiefs of Staff. As he described himself in that period, "he was the oldest, living, male ensign in Washington." However, his skill with surveys led him, immediately after the end of the war in the Pacific, to be released from active duty in the Navy to serve until June 1946 as deputy division chief with the U.S. Strategic Bombing Survey (Pacific), where he was responsible for conducting a survey of the effects of strategic bombing on civilian morale in Japan. The conclusion, which has yet to be incorporated fully into U.S. political and military thinking, was that the effects were significant but not of the expected direction.

My father returned from Japan in 1946, essentially out of the Navy, with a family to support, and limited means to do so. He had had three years of teaching experience and seven years of professional experience, but the best paying position he could find (at $4,000 a year) was as a visiting lecturer at Harvard in the fall of 1946. I received my own Ph.D. (in economics) from Yale, and, in part, for that reason I have always loved the end of this story. In the middle of the year, my father was appointed assistant professor at Harvard for the next year and received a fancy certificate to confirm that fact. However, he had informed the department chairman Merle Fainsod that he was looking for another position and wanted to be free to take it. When he later resigned from Harvard to accept a position as associate professor at Williams College, he received an excerpt from the minutes of the relevant Harvard body to the effect that he had never been appointed there. In those days, one did not turn down Harvard appointments, particularly if one did not even have a Harvard degree.

Elmo Roper, a pioneer in market research and public opinion polling, had founded the Roper Center for Public Opinion Research at Williams College (subsequently moved to the University of

Connecticut), and Williams College appointed my father, in part, to organize and to help develop programs to exploit the collection of materials that had been assembled. His background on surveys and polling also led to his being asked to join the staff of a committee of the Social Science Research Council to investigate the debacle of the alleged failure of polls to predict the outcome of the 1948 presidential election. He contributed to the resulting volume that concluded, in brief, that the pollsters stopped polling too early. (Frederick Mosteller, Herbert Hyman, Philip J. MCarthy, Eli Marks, and David B. Truman, *The Pre-Election Polls of 1948: Report to the Committee on Analysis of Pre-Election Polls and Forecasts*, New York: Social Science Research Council, 1949)

At Williams, my father continued his interest in teaching interdisciplinary courses, collaborating in teaching several courses with members of the economics department in what would now be called political economy. He also devoted his summers, primarily, to the book that he left Harvard to write, *The Governmental Process*. It was first published in 1951 while my father was a visiting professor at Columbia.

The book was substantial in coverage and length (more than 500 pages) integrating various strands of research and analysis about the U.S. political system. His former colleague and close friend, Richard E. Neustadt, writing after my father's death in 2003, described its impact and contribution for contemporary political scientists:

> When I first read *The Governmental Process* I was enormously impressed by the degree to which the world of American politics it painted was like the world I had experienced in seven years of government service, much of it in direct touch with legislation. That book is often said to have embodied

the group theory of politics. But it transcended group theorizing as previously done by making room for individuals, for individual variations, and for shifting relationships. These things Truman accomplished with three critically important concepts. He distinguished attitudes from activated interests. He distinguished "rules of the game" from lesser attitudes. And he distinguished "multiple membership" in overlapping and competing interests, moderated by the activation of those rules, as the "balance wheel" of democratic government. The sophistication of those concepts is what makes the book still relevant, after more than 50 years. (Richard E. Neustadt, "In Memoriam David B. Truman," *PS—Political Science & Politics*, Vol.37, No.1, January, 2004, p. 132)

The book was not a resounding commercial success, but it was well worth the effort to my father. Stokes records a report on a conversation my father had with my mother:

I remember saying to my wife when . . . she asked me once, "You're working awful hard on this. What do you really want out of the thing? Do you hope you are going to make a lot of money?" And I said, "No, I don't think I will" (and of course I haven't because it hasn't sold that much) but I said, "I would like it to establish me as a political scientist." And for it I hoped that it would help to give a few graduate students and young scholars who were coming along a base from which they could take off to do something different. (Donald Stokes, "David Truman," interview in Michael A. Baer, Malcolm E. Jewell, and Lee Seligman, *Political Science in America: Oral Histories of a Discipline*, Lexington, Kentucky: University Press of Kentucky, 1991, p. 145)

The intellectual success was substantial and continuing. It only recently went out of print, continues to generate income as portions of it are reprinted, and was translated into Chinese and published in

2005 as part of a series of American classics. However, my mother was frustrated in 1951 and throughout her long life that the publisher had penalized my father for the length of his manuscript by withholding his royalties for the first several thousand copies. He, of course, had exceeded the contractual number of pages and declined to cut the manuscript significantly when it was completed.

We moved to New York City and Columbia in the fall of 1950, and my parents ended up staying 19 years, most of which were extremely happy. While at Columbia, my father also taught a seminar at Yale one year, which was his fourth teaching appointment at an Ivy League institution. At the time he decided to stay at Columbia, Yale also tried to attract him. He accepted the Columbia offer in part because at Yale at the time, as at Harvard, if you did not have a degree from the institution you were considered a second-class colleague. At Columbia in 1951, he was appointed a full professor in the Department of Public Law and Government and became department chairman in 1959.

He was on sabbatical leave during the summer and first semester of 1962 when he wrote his section of a textbook on American government, which was not a great success. (Emmette S. Redford, Andrew Hacker, Alan F. Westin, and Robert C. Wood, *Politics and Government in the United States*, New York, Harcourt, Brace & World, 1965) While on sabbatical, my father was offered the deanship of Columbia College. Four and a half years later, on July 1, 1967, he became vice president and provost of Columbia University. The first building takeover would occur on April 23, 1968, fewer than ten months later.

My father loved Columbia, which was why the events described in this memoir were so painful to him. He described for Stokes in 1979 his feelings about his colleagues:

> And the other thing was that there was a marvelous group of men in that faculty who were wonderfully generous and a kind of democracy of intellect about Columbia, which I enormously respected. One was not what your credentials were. One was what one had to say. You knew you were being listened to if you had something to say, and if you didn't have anything to say it didn't make any difference what your rank was, you were going to be ignored. It was a place where one worked very hard. That was partly, of course, because Columbia has always taken its pace from this city [New York]. There's a pulse about the place that's just like the pulse you feel in midtown Manhattan. And, in that respect, it's unlike any other campus I've ever spent any time on. It's not—the pace is not that of New Haven or Princeton or Cambridge or Ann Arbor. And that can be very exciting. It also can drive you insane if you don't dilute it a little occasionally. (Stokes, p. 147)

My parents "diluted" New York City by buying a country retreat in December 1951 in Hillsdale, New York, about 100 miles and two and a half hours north of Morningside Heights. They escaped to Scrub Hill, as we call it, as many weekends and summers as they could.

I was privileged to know many of my father's Columbia colleagues. Herbert Dean lived in our apartment one year. The Richard Neustadts moved into the apartment above ours on Riverside Drive. Dick Neustadt credits my father with having found a publisher in John Wiley & Sons for his now-famous *Presidential Power* in 1960. (Neustadt, p. 132) The families continued to be very close even after Dick was called back to Harvard in 1965, following the assassination of President Kennedy, to head the Institute of Politics, which became the Kennedy School of Government. Dick Neustadt died two months after my father, and the same issue of *PS—Political Science & Politics* contains in memoriam tributes to these closest friends.

Before he became dean, my father had one other major publication that deserves mention. It was a book on the party structure and leadership in the Congress. (David B. Truman, *The Congressional Party: A Case Study*, New York, John Wiley & Sons, 1959) The book's reception was a disappointment to my father, but it is noteworthy because of the techniques he employed, including use of the computer at the Watson Laboratory at Columbia, for which my mother learned to wire the board to tell it how to do its job.

After he became dean of Columbia College, he was president of the American Political Science Association in 1965. He also brought out a second edition of *The Governmental* Process in 1971 with a new 32-page introduction.

Following the Columbia disturbances, my father accepted appointment as president of Mount Holyoke College. As part of the appointment process, he insisted that he meet with some student leaders. He subsequently received a note from them which said, "Please come." (Mary E. Tuttle, "Tribute to David Truman," Memorial Service at Mount Holyoke College, October 20, 2003, p. 1)

All was not entirely peaceful during my father's tenure at Mount Holyoke College. The Vietnam War was still going on, and many other political and societal transformations were under way. There were some building seizures, but no police "busts." During his presidency, the College decided to remain women college, a position that my father supported. He also strongly advised that his successor be a woman.

My father was honored by the Board of Trustees with the endowment of a professorship bearing his name. He was honored by some of the many students he knew at the College when the editors of the student newspaper wrote, "We will miss his sympathetic understanding, his stern acknowledgement of reality and we will perhaps never be great enough to recognize what David Truman has given us." (Tuttle, p. 2) Johnson wrote in his biographical memoir, "Truman was a rare blend of a sharp analytical intelligence with a profound amiability. As many have said, to know him is to like him. He had a ready smile and a twinkly eye that were reassuring to, for example, a young faculty member [such as Johnson] approaching him with a certain amount of awe, and even trepidation." (p. 702)

After retiring from the presidency of Mount Holyoke College in 1978 at the age of 65, my father did not immediately go into full-time retirement. During 1978-79, he was president of the Russell Sage Foundation on whose board he had served as a trustee. He was also a trustee of The Twentieth Century Fund (now The Century Foundation). He had also been a trustee of Amherst College, and twice was trustee of Hampshire College, once in his capacity of president of Mount Holyoke College and again after his retirement. Other honors included membership in the American Philosophical Society and fellow of the American Academy of Arts and Sciences.

In 1979 my parents moved permanently to Scrub Hill and lived there year-round until 1988. Previously, they spent most of the time at Scrub Hill enjoying walks on their 117 acres and were not very much involved in social or other activities in the area. Now they established deeper roots in the community. They volunteered at the local library, and my father became a trustee of the Columbia Memorial Hospital.

My father took up painting again, an activity he had spent some time doing while living in Williamstown. Johnson provides a description:

> I asked a mutual friend, painter Margot Trout, about Truman. She ran a small painting school in Great Barrington, Massachusetts, not far from the Trumans' much-loved Scrub Hill in Hillsdale, New York. After his retirement from Mount Holyoke, Truman signed up to take courses in painting. I asked Trout what struck her about him. She said there was a great modesty—a humility—about him. He approached the job without any pretense. He was, she said, a natural learner. He wanted to learn things, and he did learn things. (p. 702)

In 1988, my parents moved to Sarasota Florida and became residents of Plymouth Harbor, a continuing care retirement community. They made many new friends, and my father became a trustee of the New College Foundation. They continued to spend summers in Hillsdale, New York, though only a few weeks each summer after 1997.

In the process of completing this project, I reread my father's memoir and also a considerable amount of other material by and about him, including the Donald Stokes interview, from which I have already quoted. At the end of that 1979 interview, Stokes asked about the events at Columbia ten years earlier. My father replied:

> I'd been in that job for less than twelve months when things blew up. If you had to do things, you had to do them rapidly, and you had to make up your mind. If it was the wrong thing, it was too bad. But the ability to sit back carefully and think a thing through—uh-uh—there was not time for that.

I think that was one of the things I learned, again, about politics. I can be very compassionate about a president or a governor on the hot seat, even if he does badly, because I think I know what some of the limitations just inevitably are. You know, this is one of [the] things that I suspect has been a gain for my generation of political scientists from the depression and the war. A little more sensitive, a little more understanding of the complexities of institutions, . . . [W]e get an awful lot of simplified explanations of the complex world these days from some of our colleagues, it seems to me. (Stokes, p. 151)

I have never been in the vortex of a crisis quite the way my father was in 1968, but at the Federal Reserve and the Treasury Department I was involved in many financial crises. My father's comment in 1979, which I did not read until after his death and after I had retired from the government, rings true to me. It is one of the many lessons from this memoir.

REFERENCES

PREFACE

Jonathan Mahler, "The Year Everything Went Wrong," *New York Times Magazine*, December 28, 2003, pp. 36–37.
Paul Hond, "Stir It Up," *Columbia*, Spring 2008, pp. 12–19.

PROLOGUE

Clark Clifford, *Counsel to the President*, New York: Doubleday, 1991.

Chapter One
INTRODUCTION

"The Columbia Crisis," Transcript of a news conference with students of the Columbia School of Journalism and David B. Truman, Channel 13, WNDT-TV, May 3, 1968, 82 pp.
David B. Truman, "The Dilemmas of an Unavoidable Confrontation," Remarks for a panel of the Eighth Annual Meeting of Graduate Schools, San Francisco, December 5, 1968, 9 pp.
David B. Truman, "The Dilemmas of an Unavoidable Confrontation," abbreviated version of the preceding item, *Amherst Alumni News*, Spring 1970, pp. 2–5.
Louis Lusky and Mary H. Lusky, "Columbia in 1968: The Wound Unhealed," *Political Science Quarterly*, Vol. 84, No. 2, June 1969, pp. 169–288. Cited as Lusky and Lusky.
Crisis at Columbia: Report of the Fact-Finding Commission Appointed to Investigate the Disturbances at Columbia University in April and May 1968, New York: Random House, 1968. Cited as the Cox Commission Report or Cox.
Jerry L. Avorn and others, *Up Against the Ivy Wall: A History of the Columbia Crisis*, New York: Atheneum, 1969, by the staff of the undergraduate newspaper, *Columbia Daily Student*.
George Keller, "Six Weeks that Shook Morningside," *Columbia College Today*, Vol. 15, No. 3, Spring 1968, entire issue. Cited as *Columbia College Today*, Spring 1968.

Raymond Aron, "Student Rebellion: Vision of the Future or Echo from the Past?" *Political Science Quarterly*, Vol. 84, No. 2, June 1969, pp. 289–310.

Chapter Two
WHY COLUMBIA?

Cox Commission Report, as in chapter 1.
Frederick P. Keppel, *Columbia University*, New York: Macmillan, 1914.
New York Times, February 19, and March 6, 1946, and May 2, 1948. [Citations of the *New York Times* are listed in these references in chronological order and placed where the first such citation appears in each chapter.]
Lusky and Lusky, as in chapter 1.
"Special Report on Columbia: Part Seven," transcript of radio broadcast on WINS (New York), 7:50 a.m. and 6:15 p.m., May 16, 1968.

Chapter Three
"THE STUDENTS"—WHO WERE THEY?

New York Times, April 27, May 1, 17 and 23, and June 5 and 10, 1968.
William L. O'Neill, *Coming Apart: An Informal History of America in the 1960's*. Chicago: Quadrangle Books, 1971. It is impossible for me to resist quoting a footnote to the cited passage in O'Neill:
> To be on a troubled campus in those days was to envy the Warden and Fellows of Wadham College, Oxford. In reply to a set of non-negotiable demands, they wrote: "Dear Gentlemen: We note your threat to take what you call 'direct action' unless your demands are met immediately. We feel that it is only sporting to let you know that our governing body includes three experts in chemical warfare, two ex-commandos skilled with dynamite and torturing prisoners, four qualified marksmen in both small arms and rifles, two ex-artillerymen, one holder of the Victoria Cross, four karate experts and a chaplain. The governing body has authorized me to tell you that we look forward with confidence to what you call a 'confrontation,' and, I may say, even with anticipation." p. 291.

REFERENCES

James S. Kunen, *The Strawberry Statement: Notes of a College Revolutionary*, New York: Random House, 1969.
Irving Howe, *New York Times Magazine*, September 19, 1982.
Cox Commission Report, as in chapter 1.
Douglas M. Knight, *Street of Dreams: The Nature and Legacy of the 1960s*, Durham, North Carolina: Duke University Press, 1989.
Samuel P. Hays, "Right Face, Left Face: The Columbia Strike," *Political Science Quarterly*, Vol. 84, No. 2, June 1969, pp. 311–327.
Truman, "The Dilemmas of an Unavoidable Confrontation," as in chapter 1.
James A. Wechsler, *New York Post*, April 30, 1968.
Lusky and Lusky, as in chapter 1.
Columbia College Today, Vol. 15, No. 2, Fall 1988, pp. 30–32.
Washington Post, April 30, 1988.

Chapter Four
ENCOUNTERING PARENTS

Allen Ginsberg, *Columbia College Today*, Vol. 15, No. 2, Fall 1988, p. 32.
New York Times, May 3 and 19, 1968.
Grossner et al. v. The Trustees of Columbia University, 287 F. Supp. 535.

Chapter Five
THE FACULTY IN CRISIS

Lusky and Lusky, as in chapter 1.
Ronald Steel, *Walter Lippmann and the American Century*, New York: Vintage edition, 1981.
Cox Commission Report, as in chapter 1.
Edward Shils, "The Academic Ethos," *The American Scholar*, Vol. 47, No. 2, Spring, 1978, pp. 165–190.
David Riesman, "Commentary on Clark Kerr's Classic," Association of Governing Boards, *Reports*, March 1983.
William E. Leuchtenburg to David B. Truman, July 13, 1990, in David B. Truman papers at Mount Holyoke College.
WINS radio transcript, May 16, 1968, as in chapter 2.
New York Times, April 30, and May 1 and 2, 1968, and February 20, 1969.

Judith Shklar, "A Life of Learning," Charles Homer Haskins Lecture, American Council of Learned Societies, *Occasional Paper No. 9*, Washington, April 6, 1989.

New York Times Magazine, "The Decade that Failed," September 19, 1982.

Daniel Bell, "Columbia and the New Left," *Public Interest*, Fall 1968.

Ron Chernow, "The Cultural Contradictions of Daniel Bell," *Change*, March 1979, pp. 12–17.

Daniel Bell, *The Reforming of General Education*, New York: Columbia University Press, 1966.

Elinor Langer, "Columbia University: Still at the Crossroads," *Science*, Vol. 162, November 22, 1968, pp. 878–883.

Morris Dickstein, "Columbia Recovered," *New York Times Magazine*, May 15, 1988.

Columbia College Today, Spring 1968, as in chapter 1.

Chapter Six
THE PRESIDENCY IN CRISIS

New York Times, April 29, May 2, 6 and 14, and June 10, 1968.

Cox Commission Report, as in chapter 1.

Max Lerner, *New York Post*, May 3, 1968.

Grayson Kirk, "A Message to Alumni, Parents, and Other Friends of Columbia," June 1, 1968.

Courtney C. Brown, *The Dean Meant Business*, New York: Graduate School of Business, Columbia University, 1983.

Newsweek, May 2, 1968.

Douglas M. Knight, *Street of Dreams: The Nature and Legacy of the 1960s*, Durham, North Carolina: Duke University Press, 1989.

Chapter Seven
THE TRUSTEES AS CRISIS MANAGERS

Douglas M. Knight, *Street of Dreams: The Nature and Legacy of the 1960s*, Durham, North Carolina: Duke University Press, 1989.

Cox Commission Report, as in chapter 1.

Columbia University in the City of New York, "The Role of the Trustees of Columbia University," Report of the Special Committee Adopted by the Trustees November 4, 1957.

New York Times, April 27 and 28, and May 10, 1968.

REFERENCES

"To The Trustees of Columbia University," Confidential Memorandum from David B. Truman, February 16, 1969, in David B. Truman papers at Mount Holyoke College.
Newsweek, May 2, 1968.
David B. Truman, "Interview," Oral History Research Office, Columbia University. 1970.
"Columbia Crisis, David Truman II," Oral History Research Office, Columbia University, 1970.

Chapter Eight
THE MAYOR AND HIS ENTOURAGE

Cox Commission Report, as in chapter 1.
Lusky and Lusky, as in chapter 1.
New York Times, April 29 and 30, and May 10 and 22, 1968.

Chapter Nine
BLACK POLITICIANS ON THE SPOT

New York Times, April 25, and May 2 and 5, 1968.
Cox Commission Report, as in chapter 1.
"The Columbia Crisis," Channel 13 transcript, as in chapter 1.

Chapter Ten
THE POLICE: PRO AND CON

Cox Commission Report, as in chapter 1.
Lusky and Lusky, as in chapter 1.
New York Times, May 3, 6 and 7, and June 5, 1968.
New York Post, May 3, 1968.

Chapter Eleven
THE MEDIA: LOCAL AND NATIONAL

Jerry L. Avorn et al., *Up Against the Ivy Wall: A History of the Columbia Crisis*, New York: Atheneum, 1969, by the staff of the undergraduate newspaper, *The Student*.
Lusky and Lusky, as in chapter 1.
Columbia College Today, Spring 1968, as in chapter 1.
Grayson Kirk, "A Message to Alumni, Parents, and Other Friends of Columbia,"
June 1, 1968.

Cox Commission Report, as in chapter 1.
New York Times, April 15, 25 and 29, 1968, and January 31, 1980.
Diana Trilling, "On the Steps of Low Library," *Commentary*, Vol. 46, No. 5, November 1968, pp. 29–55.
Arnold Beichman, "David Truman of Mount Holyoke: He blew the whistle at Columbia—and learned from the experience," *Boston Globe*, November 19, 1972.
"The Columbia Crisis," Transcript of a news conference with students of the Columbia School of Journalism and David B. Truman, Channel 13, WNDT-TV, May 3, 1968, 82 pp.

Chapter Twelve
WHY 1968?

Richard Hofstadter, "The Columbia University Commencement Address of the 214th Academic Year," June 4, 1968.
William L. O'Neill, *Coming Apart: An Informal History of America in the 1960's*. Chicago: Quadrangle Books, 1971.
New York Times, May 3 and 4, 1968.
Douglas M. Knight, *Street of Dreams: The Nature and Legacy of the 1960s*, Durham, North Carolina: Duke University Press, 1989.
"The Columbia Crisis," Transcript of a news conference with students of the Columbia School of Journalism and David B. Truman, Channel 13, WNDT-TV, May 3, 1968, 82 pp.
Richard H. Adrian, "The Crisis in British Universities," The Henry LaBarre Jayne Lecture, *Proceedings of the American Philosophical Society*, Vol. 132. No. 3, September 1988, pp. 237–246.
Flora Lewis, "Look Back to Look Ahead," *New York Times*, December 27, 1985.
Nelson Lichtenstein, "A Failure that Changed the World," *New York Times Book Review*, April 3, 1988.
Cox Commission Report, as in chapter 1.
Francis Oakley, "Against Nostalgia: Reflections on Our Present Discontents in Higher Education," National Humanities Center, *Newsletter*, Vol. 12, No. 2, Spring–Summer, 1991, pp. 1-14.
Lusky and Lusky, as in chapter 1.

REMARKS AT COLUMBIA UNIVERSITY

David B. Truman, *The Governmental Process: Political Interests and Public Opinion*, New York: Knopf, 1951, second edition 1971.

REFERENCES

Robert A. McCaughey, *Stand Columbia: A History of Columbia University in the City of New York, 1754–2004*, New York: Columbia University Press, 2003.

New York Times, September 1, 2003.

David B. Truman, "Reflections on the Columbia Disorders of 1968," Columbia University Archives, 1992; revised 1995.

Richard E. Neustadt, "In Memoriam David B. Truman," *PS—Political Science & Politics*, Vol.37, No.1, January 2004, pp. 131–132.

David B. Truman, *The Congressional Party: A Case Study*, New York: John Wiley & Sons, 1959.

DAVID BICKNELL TRUMAN

David B. Truman, *The Governmental Process: Political Interests and Public Opinion*, New York: Knopf, 1951, second edition. 1971.

David B. Truman, *Administrative Decentralization: A Study of the Chicago Field Offices of the United States Department of Agriculture*, Chicago: Chicago University Press, 1940.

Richard A. Johnson, "David Bicknell Truman: 1 June 1913–28 August 2003," *Proceedings of the American Philosophical Society*, Vol. 150, No. 4, December 2006, pp. 679–702.

Frederick Mosteller, Herbert Hyman, Philip J. McCarthy, Eli Marks, and David B. Truman, *The Pre-Election Polls of 1948: Report to the Committee on Analysis of Pre-Election Polls and Forecasts*, New York: Social Science Research Council. 1949.

Richard E. Neustadt, "In Memoriam David B. Truman," *PS—Political Science & Politics*, Vol.37, No.1, January 2004, pp. 131–132.

Donald Stokes, "David Truman," interview in Michael A. Baer, Malcolm E. Jewell, and Lee Seligman, *Political Science in America: Oral Histories of a Discipline*, Lexington, Kentucky: University Press of Kentucky, 1991, pp. 135–151.

Emmette S. Redford, Andrew Hacker, Alan F. Westin, and Robert C. Wood, *Politics and Government in the United States*, New York: Harcourt, Brace & World, 1965.

David B. Truman, *The Congressional Party: A Case Study*, New York: John Wiley & Sons, 1959.

Mary E. Tuttle, "Tribute to David Truman," Memorial Service at Mount Holyoke, October 20, 2003, in David B. Truman papers at Mount Holyoke College.

Printed in the USA
CPSIA information can be obtained
at www.ICGtesting.com
LVHW041653050624
782391LV00004B/38